WHAT TO KNOW
Before YOU GO

WHAT TO KNOW
Before YOU GO

Developing the Heart
and Soul of a Missionary

DON H. STAHELI

DESERET
BOOK

SALT LAKE CITY, UTAH

To my eternal companion, Cyndy,
and to all the faithful missionaries
of the France Paris Mission, 2008–2011

Library of Congress Cataloging-in-Publication Data

Staheli, Don H., author.
   What to know before you go : developing the heart and soul of a missionary / Don H. Staheli.
      pages cm
   Includes bibliographical references and index.
   ISBN 978-1-62972-044-9 (paperbound)
   1. Mormon missionaries—Training of. 2. Mormon missionaries—Conduct of life. I. Title.
   BX8661.S68 2015
   266'.9332—dc23   2015010855

Printed in the United States of America
PubLitho, Draper, UT

10   9   8   7   6   5   4   3   2   1

CONTENTS

CONTENTS

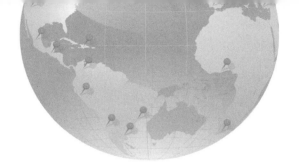

PREFACE

The messages in this book are derived from insights gained by the author through personal study and while serving as a mission president or missionary preparation instructor. The footnotes are placed at the bottoms of the pages so you can look up the references easily to continue your study. The sections titled "In Their Own Words" are true accounts written by full-time missionaries. Some of them have been edited slightly to correct grammar and to add some important context or consistency. All of the names have been changed to protect privacy.

My thanks to Sheri Dew, Jana Erickson, Emily Watts, and the wonderful staff of Deseret Book Company. Special gratitude goes to Sandy Thueson, my able secretary.

INTRODUCTION

On a hill overlooking the Seine River, not far from Paris, France, lies the old chateau (castle) where Louis XIV was born and raised. Louis was known as the Sun King. Later on in his life he built the beautiful chateau at Versailles. Adjacent to the old chateau is a large garden and forest area with beautiful flowers, expansive green lawns, and well-worn pathways through the trees. It is a jogger's paradise!

As a very busy mission president, I didn't have many opportunities to jog from the mission home up to the chateau gardens, but when the occasion presented itself, that was one of my favorite places to go, usually very early in the morning. One path through the garden leads to a gate in the old garden wall, up well-worn rock steps, and through an arched opening into the forest. There in the quiet and peaceful grove the only distraction is the occasional song of a bird or the rustle of some little animal making its way through the undergrowth. The forest is a place for thoughtful meditation.

It became my practice to follow a little trail off the main path until I arrived at a small clearing that was protected from the view of anyone passing by. In this clearing was the stump of a tree that had long since been cut down. I enjoyed sitting on this stump and thinking or praying about the missionaries, how we might improve our work, or any other thing that was weighing on my mind. Sometimes it was nice just to sit and listen to the whisper of leaves as the wind blew through the trees.

Once, while sitting on the "pondering stump," I had the distinct impression that I was not alone. I couldn't see anyone, but knew I had been joined by beings from the other side of the veil. The impression was very clear and real. My first questioning thought was who they might be. No sooner did that thought come than I received the answer. They were people who had lived in the area and had descendants still there. These were the ancestors of the people to whom we were trying to introduce the gospel. These were deceased people living in the spirit world who were being taught the gospel and were hopeful that their descendants would become converted and do their temple work. And then the second question came to mind as I wondered why they would come to me.

Again, the answer came quickly, this time as a message. Almost as if I could hear them speaking, my visitors asked that I "Tell the missionaries not to be discouraged. What they are doing really matters."

Joy filled my heart and tears welled up in my eyes as I received this encouraging message. I knew the missionaries would be equally thrilled and motivated by this important communication from beyond the veil.

Missionary work can be hard and tiring, but there is no need to be discouraged! We are getting help from sources that we cannot see but that are real and make a big difference. What we are doing is worth it to them. It really matters. They are grateful for our sacrifice and hope we will keep it up.

The purpose of this book is to give you some gospel insights that will help you be a better missionary or just a better person in general. The most important elements of good missionary work are the heart and soul of the missionary. Almost anyone can learn how to *do* missionary work. Techniques can be mastered, words can be memorized, scripture references can be learned by heart, but real missionary work is not just in the doing (as important as that is). The greatest, most effective missionaries are those who have learned how to *be* a missionary. After all, that's what we hope for new converts: not that they know everything and can do all the things a Church member can do, but that they will have the heart of a Latter-day Saint—the faith in Jesus Christ that will lead them to repentance, the desire to be baptized, a longing for the companionship of the Holy Ghost, and a commitment to obey the commandments to the best of their ability for as long as they live. The scriptures refer to that as a mighty change of heart.[1]

That's what missionaries (and all of us!) need—the heart, mind, and soul of a missionary. These will help you overcome discouragement, give you confidence in your calling, get you up in the morning even when it's dark and cold, and allow you to bear a bold testimony of the restored gospel.

So let's get started. Each chapter will give you a little better insight into some of the principles that will help you be the best missionary you can be. And whatever that is, rest assured that it will be good enough.

---

1. See Alma 5:12.

Chapter 1

YOUR DUAL NATURE

As you prepare to serve a full-time mission, one of the most important things for you to understand is the dual nature of your being. You are actually two "yous" wrapped into one. There are the inner you and the outer you. Victor Hugo, the author of the wonderful book *Les Misérables,* put it this way: "The soul helps the body, and at certain moments uplifts it. It is the only bird which sustains its cage."[1] So, you see, there are two parts to each of us—our soul or spirit (what Victor Hugo referred to as the bird) and our body (which Hugo compared to a cage).

Sometimes we pay far too much attention to the cage, and we neglect the beautiful, powerful bird that dwells inside. We stress over our physical appearance and worry that we are not good-looking enough or that we don't wear the right clothes or that our body isn't built as we would like it to be. In the process, we forget to care for our spirit, the element that gives life to our whole being. Imagine parakeet owners who spent their time shining and cleaning and worrying about the appearance

---

1. *Les Misérables: Marius* (Google Books), 70.

of the cage but neglected to feed and water the bird inside the cage. It wouldn't take long before the bird began to weaken and shrivel. The bird would soon stop singing, and the shiny cage would be almost useless. Which would you prefer to have, an expensive gilded cage with a lifeless bird, or a moderate cage with a healthy, beautiful bird? Too many people these days seem to choose the costly cage at the expense of what matters most, the bird. It is easy to see that the cage loses much of its meaning when the bird inside is too weak to sing.

People who have suffered some form of abuse in their lives are especially helped by understanding this concept. They realize that what someone else has done to them really only affected the cage. The bird inside is protected and cannot be harmed. People can mock the cage, attack the cage, abuse the cage in any way, but they cannot get to the bird inside. Even if they were to destroy the cage, the bird would just fly free.

When you understand your dual nature, you will want to care for the cage (your body) and keep it a clean and proper place for the bird (your spirit) to dwell. You will pay very close attention to the bird, to nurturing and caring for the inner you, the real source of your beautiful song.

Let's think about the real you for a moment. Imagine yourself in the premortal existence. What kind of a spirit person were you? The scriptures give us some clues. The prophet Alma taught that you were "called and prepared from the foundation of the world according to the foreknowledge of God, on account of [your] exceeding faith and good works; in the first place being left to choose good or evil; therefore [you] having chosen good, and exercising exceedingly great faith, are called with a holy calling."[2]

You were chosen by God even before you came to earth! You were one of His most faithful and obedient children. As a result of your faith and goodness, the Father decided that you would be foreordained to receive the blessings of the holy priesthood in this life. Men are ordained to the priesthood, and women receive exactly the same blessings as the men, though they have been given a complementary role and do not actually hold the keys of the priesthood in this life. That is how our Heavenly Father planned it.

Now you are living out the life that you worked for in the premortal existence. You came to earth with great hopes for yourself, determined to continue to be obedient and true to the Father. You came with confidence that you would not let yourself down, that you would be faithful to yourself. When you are tempted to do something wrong, think about who you really are and remember to be true to your real self.

It is essential that you love yourself. In fact, your ability to love others is directly dependent upon your ability to love yourself—not in a selfish or self-centered way, but with true and holy love. The Lord said, "And let every man esteem his brother as himself, and practise virtue and holiness before me. And again I say unto you, let every man esteem his brother as himself."[3] When the Lord repeats Himself in scripture, He does so because He really wants us to pay attention—what He is saying is really important. Notice that He says "as himself." In mathematics, the sign for "as" is the equal sign, so we could

2. Alma 13:3.
3. Doctrine and Covenants 38:24–25.

read this scripture "let every man esteem [love] his brother [or sister] 'equal' to himself." We should love ourselves every bit as much as we love our brother or sister—not more or less, but equal to. Having compassion for yourself—that is, kindness, forgiveness, caring, patience—is just as important as having compassion for others.

Heavenly Father loves you so much that He has given you all that can be given to a mortal person. He has provided every opportunity for you to return to His presence and to become a joint heir with His Beloved Son, Jesus Christ. That means if you do what the Father has asked of you, you will be happy now and receive all He has to offer in the next life. There you will be a king or a queen. Even if the cage isn't all you would like, the bird inside is glorious!

In Their Own Words

We met Sarah on Mother's Day at church and invited her to sit with us in sacrament meeting. After church we made an appointment to teach her. We were a little nervous because we had recently read her teaching record in the area book, which did not bear sweet tidings at all! The last time she had been seen by the missionaries she had gone storming out, yelling back to the sisters that she never wanted to see them again. With these lovely images in mind, we started our first teaching meeting with Sarah. She was so calm and seemed to take everything we said as pure truth. By the end of the meeting we had committed her to baptism. Two weeks later, she was baptized! We learned not to judge her heart too quickly.

Chapter 2

THE VOICES
THAT MATTER

In the world today, there seem to be a million voices speaking at us. We're surrounded by media of all kinds, from TV to movies to music to social contacts—voices everywhere, some good, some bad. It is helpful to know that, though we have many voices speaking *at* us, we have only three that are speaking *to* us. Understanding this will help you know to which voices you should really listen.

In reality, there are only three voices that matter. One is the voice of the Holy Ghost—the still small voice that whispers to you and speaks comfort and truth. Another is the voice of the natural man—the voice that comes from the thoughts and feelings of your mortal body. The third is the voice of your spirit—the part of you that lived in the premortal existence and will always be.

Lehi spoke of the first two voices when he taught his sons as recorded in the Book of Mormon: "And now, my sons, I would that ye should look to the great Mediator, and hearken unto his great commandments; and be faithful unto his words, and choose eternal life, according to the will of his Holy Spirit; and not choose eternal death, according to the will of the flesh and the evil which is therein, which giveth the spirit of the devil power to captivate, to bring you down to hell, that he may reign over you in his own kingdom."[1]

Now read those two verses again and substitute the word *voice* for the word *will.*

"And now, my sons, I would that ye should look to the great Mediator, and hearken unto his great commandments; and be faithful unto his words, and choose eternal life, according to the [voice] of his Holy Spirit; and not choose eternal death, according to the [voice] of the flesh and the evil which is therein, which giveth the spirit of the devil power to captivate, to bring you down to hell, that he may reign over you in his own kingdom."

When we listen to and act upon the whisperings of the Holy Ghost, we know we are doing the will of Heavenly Father. The scriptures call this "giving heed" or "hearkening" (listening *and* acting) to the Spirit. When we hearken to the Holy Ghost, we can have confidence that the Lord will take care of us.

If we listen to and act upon the voice of the flesh or "natural man,"[2] we then give power to Satan, and he will use that power to capture us and lead us into very unhappy places. When we listen to this carnal voice, we give Satan openings into which he can drive a wedge until little cracks in our behavior become big gaps. These cracks and gaps are called sins. The Holy Ghost will never lead us to sin, but by acting upon the promptings of

---

1. 2 Nephi 2:28–29 (this one is easy to remember—two voices, 2 Nephi, chapter 2).
2. Mosiah 3:19.

10

the voice of the flesh, we can be led into small transgressions that may eventually become big sins.

Actually, this happens to all of us to one degree or another. We all sin to some degree. That is part of being human. Happily, the Atonement of Jesus Christ allows us to repent. We can change our behavior and learn from our mistakes. We can look back and see how we were listening to and acting upon the whisperings of the voice of the flesh, which allowed Satan to get some power over us, and that led to our sin. Next time that voice speaks to you, you will know exactly where it will lead, so pay no attention to it.

There is a great secret that goes along with all of this—a secret that Satan doesn't want you to know, but one that Heavenly Father has revealed to us in the scriptures. It is that if you don't give in to the natural man, Satan can have no power over you. That's right! The only power Satan has is what we give to him, and we give it to him by giving heed to the voice of the natural man. With practice, we can learn to ignore that voice and give heed only to the voice of the Spirit. That's what Captain Moroni did.

In the book of Alma it says, "Yea, verily, verily I say unto you, if all men had been, and were, and ever would be, like unto Moroni, behold, the very powers of hell would have been shaken forever; yea, the devil would never have power over the hearts of the children of men."[3]

By this we know that it is possible for us to become so tuned in to the Spirit and to ignore the voice of the flesh to the point that Satan has no power over us at all. Then the Spirit becomes our main guide.

---

3. Alma 48:17.

Now, so you don't become too discouraged, please understand that this takes a very long time to achieve completely. Remember that the voice of the natural man is programmed into your mind. It is a part of you. You are hard-wired by your entrance into mortality to have that voice speaking to you nearly all the time. Just having the voice is not a sin. Even Jesus was subject to the temptations that come from the voice of the natural man. "He suffered temptations but gave no heed unto them."[4]

Sin comes only when we entertain the voice of the flesh and allow unclean thoughts and desires to take root in our mind, which will likely lead us to act upon them. Satan has only the power we allow him. There is no such thing as "the devil made me do it." We do it to ourselves, and the devil just takes advantage of our weakness.

One of the big purposes of life is to learn to listen to the Spirit and to overcome the voice of the flesh. "For the natural man is an enemy to God, and has been from the fall of Adam, and will be, forever and ever, unless he yields to the enticings of the Holy Spirit, and putteth off the natural man and becometh a saint through the atonement of Christ the Lord, and becometh as a child, submissive, meek, humble, patient, full of love, willing to submit to all things which the Lord seeth fit to inflict upon him, even as a child doth submit to his father."[5]

By the way, your body isn't always your enemy. Many promptings from the voice of the flesh are good, and attention should be paid to them. When your body says it's hungry, feed it! (Except on fast Sunday!) When you are tired, rest. Your body

4. Doctrine and Covenants 20:22.
5. Mosiah 3:19.

can give you many clues about how it should be properly used and cared for.

Listening to the third voice, the voice of your spirit, is a little more tricky. In order to hear this voice, you have to go to a level of listening that you may not be used to. This takes some practice. We are usually mindful of only two levels of awareness. The first is what we take in through our senses—see, hear, touch, taste, feel. This is the "what" level and is very basic information based on what is happening around us. The second level of awareness comes from our reaction to what we see, hear, and so forth. It is based on the thoughts and feelings that are generated by what our senses tell us. This is the "how" level—how we think and how we feel as a result of what we take in through our senses.

These first two levels of awareness determine much of what we actually do. We take in what we receive through our senses. Then, almost at the speed of light, we develop thoughts and feelings. We then act upon how we think and feel. Most of us go through life just letting the "what" and the "how" determine what we do. Think about the last time you said something you wish you hadn't. First, you heard or saw something. Then you had a thought and feeling about what you saw or heard. Then, without thinking, you spoke out. Almost immediately, you thought again and wished you had just kept quiet. This happens to all of us—so much so that we have little sayings to help us fix it, such as, "Think twice before you speak," or, "On second thought . . ." Practicing a deeper level of awareness will make what you say and do more meaningful and more in line with the true desires of your heart.

The third level of awareness is the "why" level. When you venture into this deeper level of listening, you go beyond the messages of your senses and superficial thoughts and feelings, to where the "real you" is speaking. Here you will find a voice that speaks to why things are the way they are and why you are here on earth. The voice of your spirit comes from the real you, not the you that you see in the mirror, which is influenced so heavily by the voice of the flesh. This is the voice that is speaking when you are offering a sincere prayer and feel that you are really being heard by Heavenly Father. You will also hear this voice when you are bearing a sincere testimony of the gospel or any time you are speaking under the influence of the Holy Ghost. It is the voice of the you that knows but has come through the veil of forgetfulness.

Remember, you have always existed. You existed in a form we call intelligence.[6] Heavenly Father then provided you with a spirit body.[7] You were an obedient and faithful daughter or son of God. That person who was so good in the premortal existence is still with you. It *is* you! You came to earth with great expectations and hope that you would continue to be faithful, that you wouldn't let yourself down. If you take a little time and quietly listen to this part of you, you will come to understand the "why" of things and will regain some of the vision that you must have had before you entered mortality. Then you will say and do things that are pleasing to the real you, the eternal you, not just act on how you feel or think at the moment.

You can hear the voice of the inner you by sitting quietly, clearing your mind as best you can of the stresses of the day, and then listening not to the superficial thoughts that will come, but to the deeper thoughts that reflect your true spiritual

6. See Abraham 3:21–22.
7. See Ether 3:16–17.

THE VOICES THAT MATTER

self. We call this pondering or meditation. President David O. McKay said, "Meditation is a form of prayer. . . . Meditation is one of the most secret, most sacred doors through which we pass into the presence of the Lord."[8] As with most things, you'll get better at this as you practice.

Again, how do voices work? First, the will of the Lord for you will be communicated through the voice of the Spirit, which will speak to your mind and to your heart[9] and help you know what to do.[10] By acting upon the enticings (the voice) of the Holy Ghost, "ye may know the truth of all things."[11] The Holy Ghost will never let you down.

Second, you will hear the voice of the flesh telling you to do something that will lead you away from the Lord. This might be something relatively innocent, like a suggestion that you sleep in when you should be getting up, watch a movie with inappropriate content, eat or drink something that isn't good for you, or whatever. If you give in to these little promptings of the natural man, you will slowly but surely give "the spirit of the devil power to captivate, to bring you down to hell, that he may reign over you in his own kingdom,"[12] because little sins almost always lead to bigger ones.

Third, if you listen quietly and carefully, you will hear the voice of your spirit. This voice will be a source of wisdom and will reveal the true desires of your heart.

In spite of all the noise and chaos that surround you and the voices that speak *at* you, there are only three voices that

---

8. *Teachings of Presidents of the Church: David O. McKay* (2011), 32.

9. See Doctrine and Covenants 8:2.

10. See 2 Nephi 32:5.

11. Moroni 10:5.

12. 2 Nephi 2:29.

really have power to speak *to* you. Pay attention to the voice of the flesh, and you open the door for Satan to come in. This voice leads to unhappiness now and an eternity out of God's presence. Listen to the Holy Ghost and the voice of your eternal spirit, and you will not go wrong. These lead to happiness in this life and the joy of eternal life, which is life with Heavenly Father. Listen and choose the right!

In Their Own Words

One of the greatest miracles I saw happened with an investigator named Deborah. She had been investigating the Church for several months and had set a goal to be baptized, but she did not feel worthy to make a covenant like that. Her entire life, she had felt a hatred of herself, which was worsened by her bad health. One Sunday, Deborah had to leave church right before sacrament meeting, because of illness. She later told us that she was beating herself up for not being able to stay at church. This continued until she walked up to her front door, when all of a sudden she felt the great love of the Savior for her and, for the first time in her life, a love for herself. When she told us of this experience, she was so happy and the Spirit was very strong. Deborah was soon baptized and is now a strong member of the branch.

Chapter 3

THE POWER OF REPENTANCE

In the Book of Mormon, Captain Moroni is referred to as a mighty man of God.[1] There is no more heroic picture than that of Captain Moroni standing with the Title of Liberty. In the Book of Mormon, right after we are told of the greatness of Moroni,[2] additional examples are given of men equal in righteousness and power. These exemplary men are none other than Ammon, Aaron, Omner, Himni, and Alma the Younger. Why is that surprising? Because those men had been among the vilest of sinners. They were all guilty of trying to destroy the Church and of committing spiritual murder.[3] As far as we know, Moroni did none of these things. How did the former sinners come to be compared with the righteous Book of Mormon hero Moroni? They repented! Yes, repentance, when done correctly, really works!

---

1. See Alma 48:11.
2. See Alma 48:17.
3. See Alma 36:14.

The Lord told the Prophet Joseph Smith, "Behold, he who has repented of his sins, the same is forgiven, and I, the Lord, remember them no more."[4] And He meant it! You are almost certainly not capable of committing a sin from which you cannot ultimately gain complete forgiveness. Make no mistake, there is a price to pay for sin, there are consequences, but forgiveness is always available to those who truly seek it.

"Come now, and let us reason together, saith the Lord: though your sins be as scarlet, they shall be as white as snow; though they be red like crimson, they shall be as wool."[5] That is no ordinary man speaking, not even a prophet, but the Lord Himself. Our task is to believe Him and to take full advantage of His Atonement.

All sins require confession. The Lord said, "By this ye may know if a man repenteth of his sins—behold, he will confess them and forsake them."[6] Most sins need only be confessed to God in prayer. The more serious sins must be confessed to your priesthood leader. When in doubt, go to your bishop and talk to him. You can trust him fully. He will guide you with loving kindness and help in the repentance process.

Be open and truthful with your bishop and stake president. Leave nothing out just because you are embarrassed. Whatever you do, don't go into the mission field with unresolved sins. That will result in serious consequences and could even require that you go home early.

Some people who have committed serious sin feel like they can never really be forgiven. It may well be true that the

---

4. Doctrine and Covenants 58:42.

5. Isaiah 1:18.

6. Doctrine and Covenants 58:43.

victims of their sin may have a hard time forgiving, and they may struggle to forgive themselves, but the Lord will definitely forgive. He stands ready to accept the broken heart and contrite spirit (the sincere desire to repent) of all who offer these to Him. His love knows no bounds. He has already paid the price for your sin. All you have to do is repent and He will attribute to you a portion of His suffering. His sacrifice will count for you, justice will be served, and you will be clean. You will be as clean as Moroni, and Satan's power to deceive you will be greatly diminished.

Notice in Alma 48:19 where the Lord speaks of those missionaries who "were no less serviceable unto the people than was Moroni." What put them on a level equal to Moroni? What did they do to deserve such a classification? After they repented, "They did preach the word of God, and they did baptize unto repentance all men whosoever would hearken unto their words." Repent and teach the gospel, and the Lord will consider you equal to one such as Moroni. You will be just as helpful to the Lord as he was.

In Their Own Words

After I had been in the mission field for only about six months, my mission president decided to put me with another elder who, like me, had been in the mission field for only six months. We were assigned to work in Calais, a small coastal city in the north of France. My companion and I were excited to work together, but we soon realized that our ability to speak French and communicate with the people was not as good as we had wished. Up until this point, we both had served only with elders who spoke the language fluently and who had been in the mission longer than us. Despite the odds against us, my companion and I were ready to get to work and baptize every soul in Calais.

We talked to people in the streets and on the roads. We talked to people on the buses and trains. We went to homes and into apartment buildings to knock on people's doors. We purified our lives and lived the mission rules perfectly in hopes that the Lord would direct us to someone who was searching for our message.

After weeks of searching, we hit rock bottom. This was not the first time we were discouraged, but this was the first time we wanted to give up. We were in the middle of contacting one day when we decided we were done! We hung our heads and headed back to our apartment. I remember thinking that we couldn't do it anymore. Our inability to communicate in the native language was preventing us from sharing our message. My companion and I were convinced our mission president was wrong in putting us together, so we decided to call our zone leader and tell him that we couldn't do it anymore; we needed to be put with more experienced companions.

Our zone leader answered our phone call and wondered what we were doing calling him in the middle of the day. We told him of our situation and distress. He told us to get up and to go back outside. He told us that the Lord would guide us and we would find someone to teach. He said, "The Lord always keeps His promises."

We were not happy with our zone leader's counsel, but we slowly got up and dragged ourselves back outside. We decided we would take the bus and try an area on the other side of town. We didn't even make it out the front door of our apartment complex when I felt the phone in my pocket vibrate. I didn't recognize the number, but when you're a missionary you answer any call that comes to your phone. I answered the phone and was greeted by a Frenchman who called himself Pierre. Pierre told me that he was an old investigator and that missionaries had taught him a few years earlier. He insisted that we come to his house to teach him. My companion and I went from being the two most discouraged elders to the two most motivated in all of Europe.

We took the train and met Pierre at his house. He was patient with us and did not care that our French was broken. We got to know Pierre and found out his beliefs and what he had already known of the Church. When we left his house, we were awestruck. We boarded the train back to our city and were so happy to have finally found someone to teach. We called our zone leader to tell him of the great news. He told us to remember what he had said earlier, "The Lord always keeps His promises."

Chapter 4

JUSTIFICATION AND SANCTIFICATION

The doctrine of justification and sanctification can be hard to understand. It is very important, however, to know how these two great principles are applied in your life and in the lives of those whom you will teach as a full-time missionary. Perhaps the following parable will help your understanding.

A young boy received a new pair of pants. The first time he wore them, his mother firmly reminded him that they were new and he should be careful not to get them dirty. Of course, she knew he would not be able to keep them completely clean, and she had the means to wash them clean again, but she wanted him to learn to treat his things nicely and to make choices that would keep them as clean as possible. So, the boy went out to play in his new pants.

A short time later, the boy came home and, sure enough, his new pants had stains on the knees. He was very sorry he had gotten his new pants dirty and expressed his feelings to his mother. "I'm so sorry that I got my pants dirty," he said. "Are they ruined forever, Mother?"

"No," his mother replied. "I can wash them clean."

And so his mother washed the pants clean and gave them back to the boy to wear again. But when he put them on, he noticed that they still had some stain on the knees. "Mother," he said, "I can't wear these pants, there is still stain on the knees. They're not clean."

"Don't worry, Son," said the wise woman. "I know there is still some stain, but you can wear the pants. They are clean. It will take several more washings to completely remove the stains, but in the meantime, you can wear them. They are clean."

So it is with us. The Father sent us to our new earth experience with the solemn commandment that we should avoid sin. At that point, we were completely clean from sin. He knew, however, that we could not always remain clean, so He provided the wonderful cleansing power of the Atonement wrought by His Beloved Son, Jesus Christ. When we approach the Father to confess our sins and admit before Him that we are not clean, we may have the feeling that, because of our sin, we are ruined and lost forever. Our loving Father assures us that we are not ruined and that He will provide the means whereby we can be clean again.

As the Atonement is applied in our behalf, we are made clean—that is, we are justified. Unfortunately, we may still have the memory of our sins; we may feel stained and not worthy of the Lord's blessing. We might pray, "Father, I cannot serve Thee, for I am still stained by sin." His response will be, "Don't worry, Daughter. Do not be concerned, Son. I know there is still some stain, but you can serve. You are clean. It will take some time and further repentance to completely remove the stains, for you to be sanctified, but in the meantime, you can serve. You are clean enough."

Justification comes by repentance, baptism, and the gift of the Holy Ghost. We are then cleansed from sin. Through continued repentance and obedience, we remain pure, even though we are not perfect. By the ongoing application of the Atonement—that is, by the cleansing blood of Jesus Christ—all the stains of our sin will eventually be removed and we will be sanctified. Then we will be completely clean and worthy to live in the presence of God, "for there can no man be saved except his garments are washed white; yea, his garments must be purified [justification] until they are cleansed from all stain [sanctification], through the blood of him [Jesus Christ] of whom it has been spoken by our fathers, who should come to redeem his people from their sins."[1]

"For by the water [baptism] ye keep the commandment; by the Spirit ye are justified [receive a remission of sins], and by the blood [the Atonement] ye are sanctified [made completely clean]."[2]

Even though you have sinned and been to some degree unclean, through repentance you should feel confident that Heavenly Father will accept you as His servant. Your bishop and stake president will judge your behavior to determine if your repentance has been adequate. They will be wise and loving in their judgment. If they say you are clean, then you can believe them, and you can serve with complete confidence. You will be just as worthy as anyone else.

Another important way to know that you are justified by the Lord is to feel the companionship of the Holy Ghost. If you can feel the Spirit, you know the Lord has accepted your

1. Alma 5:21.
2. Moses 6:60.

repentance and you are justified. Just keep up the good work and you will, through the grace of Jesus Christ and in the due time of the Lord, be sanctified and fit to live forever in the presence of the Father and the Son.

In Their Own Words

We were sitting in a lesson with one of our progressing investigators. He hadn't taken a drink of alcohol in two months after we committed him to live the Word of Wisdom. We knew his biggest concern with committing to a baptismal date was that he was afraid to be baptized until he was strong enough to always resist the temptation to drink. Both my companion and I felt strongly that he was ready to be baptized. We studied up and gave him a good lesson on baptism and the gift of the Holy Ghost. At the end of the lesson, I invited him to be baptized. He was quiet for about twenty seconds, and we were sure he was going to say yes. Finally, he said, "I think I want to wait." I sat quietly shocked that, despite the Spirit that was present, he had said no.

My companion started talking and my mind started racing. "Should we push or should we just let him wait?" I started praying silently to know what to do. Abruptly, my companion stopped talking and turned and looked at me. Later that day he told me that he suddenly had the thought, "Let your companion talk." Instantly, both my companion and our investigator were just looking at me! I was quiet for a second and then I asked him how his reading was going. He said he had just finished 2 Nephi 32. Idea! I said, "So, you just read about the gospel, the doctrine of Christ. That's just like 3 Nephi 27. Let's go there." We read about how the Holy Ghost cleanses us and talked about what that means. As we read, I knew he needed to be baptized, and I knew it needed to be in three weeks. We talked about how wanting to be sure he was strong enough to resist temptation was good, because it showed how seriously he took his future baptismal covenant. Then we read Alma 7:14–15 about how we should "fear not" and be baptized "this day." I bore my testimony to him about baptism and the Holy Ghost and told him that we really felt he needed to be baptized in three weeks. I said, "Will you be baptized on December 4th?" He sat quietly with a furrowed brow, and finally responded, "I'll do it!"

Chapter 5

CAPABILITY, RESPONSIBILITY, ACCOUNTABILITY

Some sinful behavior can be very hard to overcome. This is especially true for those actions that are habit-forming or addictive. Obviously, drug abuse would be in this category. So is sexual sin. As a member of the Church and a novice disciple of Jesus Christ, you have promised not to be involved in sexual activity outside the bonds of marriage. Even then, care must be taken, but before marriage you must be especially careful. Some people say that sexual behavior that does not involve another person is okay and is just a way to release tension. This is not true. Such behavior can be addictive and can lead to more serious sin. That is one of the most troubling things about addiction. It often starts rather innocently with behavior that is "not so bad," but soon that behavior is not enough, so something more exciting or stimulating is tried.

The viewing or reading of pornographic material is definitely a form of sexual sin. In some ways, it is among the most dangerous of such behaviors. It can and often does lead to more destructive and self-defeating actions. If a person continues to seek out or fails to avoid exposure to pornography, it can rapidly become a very serious and habitual problem. As difficult as it may be, if you have experienced this or any other form of sexual sin, speak to a parent, a priesthood leader, or some other trusted person, and make sure you don't get wrapped up in the chains of a very bad habit.

Let's talk about three particular things to consider as you work to overcome self-defeating behaviors. First is your *capability*. This means your knowledge of right and wrong and your increasing ability to avoid doing what you know you shouldn't do. The more you study the gospel and keep trying to do what's right, the more knowledge you will gain about how to live a Christlike life. Your knowledge of good and evil will become refined, and you will be more and more capable of choosing the right. For example, when unclean thoughts come into your mind, you will know that they should not be allowed to stay, so you will start singing a hymn or quoting a scripture to yourself, or doing some other little thing that helps you stay clean. Thus, you will become more capable of overcoming a bad habit.

The second thing to consider is your *responsibility*. You have made promises that you will keep the commandments and that you will live a clean and wholesome life. These promises were made at your baptism and when you received other priesthood ordinances. Remember when you were interviewed and the bishop asked you questions about your worthiness? When you told him you were worthy, you weren't just talking about the past and the present, you were promising to be worthy in the future, too. Once you receive your temple endowment, these promises become even more serious and sacred.

CAPABILITY, RESPONSIBILITY, ACCOUNTABILITY

When we make promises, the Lord and His servants (the bishop, the stake president, the mission president, and so on) expect us to keep them. We have our agency and can choose to break our promises, but we really have no right to do so. The Lord has every right to expect us to live up to our responsibilities.

One day you may get a loan from the bank to buy a car or a house. The bank will require you to promise to pay the money back. If you break your promise, the bank will take back the home or the car. They won't let you keep it. Sure, you can stop making payments on the loan, but you really have no right to do so, because you promised you would live up to your responsibility and pay what is owed.

We owe everything to the Lord. He expects us to live up to our responsibility to Him. If we do so, He will bless us and fulfill all the promises He has made to those who are obedient. He has said, "I, the Lord, am bound when ye do what I say; but when ye do not what I say, ye have no promise."[1] When we remember our responsibility to the Lord and to those who are counting on us, we will receive power to do the right thing.

Third, think about your *accountability.* You will be held accountable for your actions. This ought to scare you a little bit and motivate you a lot to choose the right. Your bishop and stake president have interviewed or will interview you to help you prepare to serve a worthy mission. Your mission president will interview you at least four times per year to offer help and guidance as you strive to stay worthy. Temple recommend interviews will come around every two years for the rest of your life, to give you the opportunity to account for your behavior

---

1. Doctrine and Covenants 82:10.

and to declare your worthiness. Each of these interviews is like a mini-judgment day, in preparation for the Final Judgment that will take place sometime after this life. If we can give a good accounting of ourselves throughout our earth life, the final accounting will be a pleasant and joyful experience.

Most of the time, missionaries who are trying to overcome a bad habit focus almost entirely on increasing their capability. This is great, but it may not be enough. If you will remember your promises, your sacred responsibility to do good and to avoid bad behavior, and consider that you will be held accountable for choosing the right, you will be even more motivated to be worthy and to keep the covenants you made at baptism and in the holy temple.

Another thing you may find helpful is to remember that people are praying for you. Your loved ones, friends, and priesthood leaders are praying that you will be the kind of missionary they know you can be. And somewhere, probably unknown to you now, there is a young lady or young man who is praying that you will live so as to be worthy to go with her or him to the temple to be sealed for time and all eternity. Live worthily for yourself, but also strive to live up to the hopes and dreams others have for you. The Lord will bless you as you strive not to let yourself or others down.

Remember capability, responsibility, and accountability. These three combined will serve you well in your efforts to be a worthy missionary.

In Their Own Words

It was my first area in the mission. We were teaching a small family who became curious about the Church after seeing the impact it had on their relatives. Charles, the father, was a bus driver whose life consisted of alcohol, tobacco, and tattoos. He wanted to change. He wanted to be an example for his two young boys. After almost two months of teaching his family they all agreed to be baptized. The father grew very nervous. He knew that in order to get baptized he would have to give up his addiction to smoking. We were there to help.

I was really struggling with the language and could only speak a few words at a time. However, I felt a strong connection to Charles. It was like we had so much to tell each other, but I couldn't speak, nor could I understand him.

As the day approached when he would give up smoking in its entirety my trainer proposed that we give him a blessing. We asked him who he would prefer administer the blessing. Without much thought and tears in his eyes he pointed at me. I became overwhelmed with fear that slowly transitioned into confidence. I placed my hands on his head, giving him his first-ever priesthood blessing. Silence filled the room. The French flowed simply but smoothly. The next time I would offer a priesthood prayer for Charles would be on the day of his baptism, standing next to him, all dressed in white. His wife and two young boys would follow his example. At last, I realized this mission wasn't some joke. Somebody sent me here for a reason. Almost like a needle in a haystack, I found a friend for life.

Chapter 6

DO YOUR DUTY

The following occurred during the dedication of the Preston England Temple. I was there on a work assignment and noticed a man who was serving as a volunteer security guard in the building where President Gordon B. Hinckley and Sister Marjorie P. Hinckley were staying.

He looked a little pitiful sitting by himself at the end of the long corridor. A rather small Englishman with thin and scruffy hair, Leslie was a security guard in a building associated with the temple near Preston, England, a building that had a few too many security guards. I'm not sure what they expected would render the place insecure, but whatever it was, they were certainly prepared. The guards were placed with a strategy designed, I suppose, to fend off whatever evil might lurk in the hearts of calculating men. And Leslie must have been assigned his post as an integral part of some grand defensive tactic.

The truth is, Leslie was guarding a locked door at the end of a little-used hallway. Why, I cannot say. No bare-handed human could get through the heavy, bolted door. Whatever could break it down, should someone for some unknown reason want to break it down, would not be deterred by diminutive Leslie. The main threat from this direction was not likely to be from any outside source of danger, but from the almost deadly boredom that filled the air at the end of the hall such that I didn't know how Leslie could breathe.

I could not help but feel sorry for this poor man. I introduced myself, hoping a moment of conversation might ease the monotony some.

"And your name?" I asked.

"Leslie," he said quietly, perhaps a little annoyed at my intrusion.

"And where are you from, Leslie?"

"Liverpool."

"Ah," I quipped, "Leslie of Liverpool."

He grinned a bit sheepishly and probably thought I was making fun of him.

Leslie was very pleasant, though, and quickly my impression of him grew quite positive. Here was a bright, middle-aged man with a family to care for. He wasn't a big man, but not quite as small as I had first thought.

I soon learned that Leslie was a volunteer. Yes, he worked as a security guard in another city, in Liverpool, actually, but his current post was manned as a matter of dedicated service.

"Leslie," I said, "could I get you a softer chair?"

"No," said he, "this one will do."

"Well," I proposed, "do you really need to be here? Nothing seems likely to happen."

He looked around as if to quickly assess the current level of security.

"I'll just do what I've been asked," he said in his thick Liverpudlian accent. "I'll just do me duty."

"May I at least bring you a can of juice or something? You could man your post and still drink some juice."

"No, thanks," he replied with a certain firmness in his voice. "I'll just do me duty."

I finally gave up. "Okay, have a good evening," I said in parting. I admit I was not very sympathetic to Leslie's sense of duty. He seemed a bit overzealous to me.

That night I had an interesting dream. I was in England, so it is not surprising that it was a dream of knights and heavy armor and white chargers. There were brave fighting scenes and charging hordes and clanging swords.

One knight stood out among all the rest. I don't remember if his armor was actually shining, but he was strong and true and the hero of my dream.

As the hero-knight emerged victorious, he stopped and dismounted his powerful steed. He stood before me, removed his helmet with dignity, and quietly introduced himself.

"Good day, sir," he said calmly. "I am Leslie, Leslie of Liverpool."

I awoke with a start. Wide awake. And I saw clearly the courage of Leslie.

He had been asked to perform a rather perfunctory task, but his sense of honor and duty caused him to do it to the very best of his ability. I think he would have guarded the Royal Jewels with no more pride or careful attention. Even as a volunteer, not being paid at all and sitting alone in that empty hall, he felt a commitment to muster all his professional skill and to focus on the performance of his duty. Even with distractors and detractors like me around, he was determined to stay on track and do it right.

Leslie taught me that to do your duty is to set aside self

and give heart and mind to the higher good. It is the Leslies of the world, each one doing his or her duty, that allow us all to rise above our natural human meanness and achieve what none could do alone. To give it your all, even when the individual task seems routine and almost meaningless—that is the fulfillment of duty.

The next evening as I was leaving the building I looked in hope for Leslie. He was there again, at the end of the hall, a knight in invisible armor doing his duty. I was glad to see him. We greeted each other. I didn't tell him why, but I asked a passerby to take my picture standing next to Leslie. I wanted to remember what a hero looks like and to prove that I had known one.

"I'll just do me duty." That's the stuff of real power. Lancelot, Gawain, and Galahad are legendary knights known for cunning and strength, but Leslie of Liverpool, the great doer of duty, is my hero.

In Their Own Words

It was the first Monday of a new transfer [a "transfer" is the six-week period between missionary assignments to new areas] and we had not been able to schedule a meeting for that night. We didn't know what to do, so we got on our knees to ask the Lord. As we were working and planning by the Spirit, we received some guidance. My companion saw in his mind's eye a man with facial hair, wearing blue jeans, standing next to a park by a bus stop. I was impressed we should go to a certain subway stop and that there would be some buildings nearby. We went out to find this man, but when we arrived at our destination, no one was in sight. Nevertheless, we contacted everyone we could find.

Just as we were about to go back to our apartment, a man came around the corner. We stopped him, had a great conversation, gave him a copy of the Book of Mormon, and made a follow-up appointment. At the end of the contact, we smiled as we noticed that the man had a beard and was wearing blue jeans, and we were next to a park by a bus stop. And there were buildings across the street! Our prayers were answered.

Chapter 7

UNFOLD AND SIMPLIFY

When teaching the gospel to friends of the Church or investigators, it is vital to remember that their understanding of certain words and doctrines may be quite different from your own. The knowledge you take for granted and even the vocabulary you use may be completely foreign to them. When you speak of Heavenly Father, they are processing what you say in terms of their personal perception of God. Almost certainly, that perception will be different from yours and perhaps far from the truth. When you teach about priesthood, most people will think in terms of the person, not the power. That is, they see the "priesthood" as their pastor or priest, and likely do not think of the concepts of power, authority, and keys. So if you teach of priesthood keys, they may think of the keys used by the minister to open the church building. When you teach of the Holy Ghost, heaven knows what they will imagine. Prayer, for many, is not a personal conversation with God, but a set of written expressions to be repeated over and over. What you are teaching may not be what they are hearing.

It is very important, therefore, that you teach to their level of understanding, not yours.

First you have to establish what they know and understand. You can then decide how to gear your teaching. You do this by asking simple questions, such as, "When you think of God, how do you imagine Him to be?" Or you could ask, "When you pray, how do you go about it?" Or, "When you hear the word *prophet*, what does that mean to you?"

To be sure you understand the investigator's response, you can then ask a clarifying question or make a simple statement, and repeat back what you heard them say, such as, "So, when you think of God, you think of an intangible, spiritual essence?" Or, "What I hear you saying is that, for you, a prophet is like a bearded old man who calls down the curses of heaven on wicked people." The investigator can then either confirm that you got it right or restate his or her thoughts to correct your impression. You can repeat the process, if necessary. In the end, you will have a good understanding of the person's knowledge, and in turn the investigator will feel like you are listening and trying to understand him or her.

When people have trusted you enough to reveal their private thoughts and feelings, it is a nice idea to thank them for sharing by saying something like, "Thank you for sharing your thoughts about prayer. It is obviously an important part of your life." Then follow up with an introduction to your teaching, such as, "May we share with you what we have learned about this sacred experience?" Or, "Would you like to know what a modern-day prophet has said about prayer?" Now they know you understand them, they have given you permission to teach, and you know at what level of understanding to begin.

In *Preach My Gospel* is a wonderful quote from President

John Taylor that says, "It is true intelligence for a man to take a subject that is mysterious and great in itself, and to unfold and simplify it so that a child can understand it."[1] Think about unfolding something. You just reveal one layer at a time until the whole thing is open and easy to see. We unfold by teaching one part or principle at a time, and we simplify by not making things too complicated for our investigator to understand. Simplifying means teaching at the level of understanding of the one being taught.

A beautiful example of this is found in the Book of Mormon in Alma, chapter 18. Here Ammon, having already gained the trust of King Lamoni, was given the opportunity to teach the gospel to the king. Ammon was wise and well prepared. He was not seen by the king as a threat, but as "harmless" (v. 22). Ammon had a plan, a strategy for teaching King Lamoni, which he exercised to perfection (see v. 23).

Ammon began with a very simple question, "Believest thou that there is a God?" He quickly learned the level of King Lamoni's understanding when the king replied, "I do not know what that meaneth." Ammon was using vocabulary unfamiliar to the king, so he rephrased the question in a more simple fashion: "Believest thou that there is a Great Spirit?" Now he was on the king's level, as confirmed by the answer, "Yea." Ammon then began the unfolding process by teaching, "This is God" (vv. 24–28). King Lamoni now understood that the Great Spirit, of whom he seemed to have known something, is God. Ammon then proceeded to "unfold and simplify" the gospel of Jesus Christ, and the king was converted.

---

1. *The Gospel Kingdom*, sel. G. Homer Durham (1943), 270; as quoted in *Preach My Gospel: A Guide to Missionary Service* (2004), 182.

A fun exercise to practice simplifying your gospel teaching is to take a word like *priesthood*, or *gospel*, or *prophet*, and define it in five words or fewer. For example, a simple definition of *prophet* might be "messenger of God." When you teach about prophets, you can say something like, "Joseph Smith was a prophet, a messenger of God." When you "unfold and simplify," even "a child can understand" your message.

In Their Own Words

For my first assignment in the mission field, I was assigned to work in a city where the work was struggling a little bit. We had high hopes of getting things back on track, but seeing a baptism there seemed out of the question. During my second week, we went to a zone training where our mission president felt inspired to tell us that every companionship could baptize by the end of the year. I was shocked and surprised because, quite frankly, it was approaching the end of the year and we had no one to work with.

On the ride back to our city I sat pondering how we could baptize someone if we had no progressing investigators or even potential investigators, when suddenly we received a phone call from a member whose name we didn't recognize. He was a recently returned missionary from our area whose mother had become interested in the Church and had started asking him questions. We set up an appointment to meet with her and from the very beginning felt a special spirit. On our second appointment we invited her to be baptized and she accepted. Several weeks later, what seemed impossible had become a reality and she was baptized. It wasn't easy and there were times I was scared it wouldn't work out, but we went forward with faith and, with the help of the Lord, we were able to bring a daughter of God into His Church.

Chapter 8

OVERCOMING DISTRACTIONS

It doesn't take much to cripple a powerful jet engine. A five-cent nut or bolt can cause severe damage to an engine costing millions. All it takes is for someone to drop some Foreign Object Debris (abbreviated FOD—pronounced "fawd") on the runway of an airport or the deck of an aircraft carrier, and the tremendous force of the jet engine sucking air into its intake may gulp the FOD. When the FOD hits the jet's fan blades, which are spinning at thousands of revolutions per minute, terrible damage can be done very quickly. Even a little FOD can cause a lot of damage!

As we go spinning through life, there is plenty of Foreign Object Debris in our path. This is not the nuts or bolts or other stuff left behind by a careless jet-engine mechanic, but the kind of rubbish that can do severe damage to our mind and spirit. The foreign objects that get put in our way might be the dirty lyrics of a song, a suggestive scene in a movie, the profanity we hear at school or work, pornography of any kind, financial debt, bullying, and on and on. There seems to be plenty of such debris all around, and it can do real damage.

Just like a jet engine, our intake will suck up whatever comes into our path. We take in things through our eyes and ears, and whatever comes in is quickly processed in our brain and becomes a permanent fixture in our mind. We have to manage a small amount of FOD; it's almost impossible to avoid. But if we take in too much, or if we absorb *any* on purpose, the damage can be severe and very difficult to overcome.

Missionary FOD comes in the same forms as are harmful to others, but missionaries seem to be far more sensitive to it and more easily damaged. A missionary can't function without the companionship of the Holy Ghost, the Spirit of the Lord. The Spirit will not tolerate FOD, and if a missionary gives in to temptation and takes in damaging debris, the Spirit will leave. Mission rules give guidelines that, if obeyed, will protect a missionary from FOD.

It would be good to make use of a new kind of FOD:

F—Faith
O—Obedience
D—Diligence

This kind of FOD comes from the Lord and will build you up and yield blessings of success and happiness.

Faith in the Lord Jesus Christ is the beginning of all blessings, the first step in building a testimony, and the foundation of all the ordinances of salvation. It is the first principle of the gospel of Jesus Christ. It is the ultimate reason for all we do in the Church and all the good we do for others. A faithful missionary trusts in Jesus Christ and works through the day with hope and optimism. He or she studies about Jesus, prays about Jesus, bears testimony of Him, and remembers Him always.[1]

Obedience has been called the first law of heaven. All blessings are predicated or based on our obedience.[2] If we obey, we are blessed. If we are disobedient, we are not eligible for the blessing. It's almost as simple as that. Occasionally, people are blessed even when they don't seem to deserve it, but that's often based on someone else's need, not the worthiness of the disobedient one. In the end, the disobedient person will fail. It's better to be obedient and not risk losing the blessings. An obedient missionary keeps all the mission rules with exactness. Such a missionary never leaves her or his companion and always acts like a servant of God.

Diligence is the key to most success. Rarely does anything good come to those who are not diligent. To be diligent is to stick to the task and work hard, doing your very best even though it is difficult and success is long in coming. A diligent missionary plans the day well (including a backup plan), seeks the guidance of the Holy Ghost, talks to everyone he or she can, and doesn't quit.

Lehi and his family understood these principles as they learned the workings of the Liahona, their guiding compass. Nephi wrote, "And it came to pass that I, Nephi, beheld the pointers which were in the ball, that they did work according to the *faith* and *diligence* and heed [*obedience*] which we did

---

1. See 2 Nephi 25:26.
2. See Doctrine and Covenants 130:20–21.

give unto them."[3] When sin and other distractions got in the way, the Liahona wouldn't work. Only by paying attention to the divine form of FOD could Lehi and his family be guided.

If you would like a spiritual compass to guide your efforts, get rid of the silly or sinful Foreign Object Debris in your life. Do all you can to develop your personal commitment to uplifting and heavenly FOD (faith, obedience, and diligence).

In Their Own Words

My companion and I were on the train one evening after a meeting had fallen through. We noticed a young man looking at us, so I pointed to my missionary name tag and asked if he knew about the Church. He asked us to tell him the story of Jesus. My companion gave him a brief lesson and we scheduled a meeting for the next Friday. We planned to meet him at a train stop and then find a quiet place to visit with him. He didn't have a phone, so we had no way to reconfirm before our appointment, but we saw him on the train that morning. When he saw us, he said, "Hey, Sisters! Seven o'clock tonight, right?" We were so excited!

All day long we had a skip in our step as we anticipated meeting with him that evening. Incredibly, he didn't show up at the scheduled time, but about an hour later he found a phone and called to reschedule. We saw him the next Sunday and a week later invited him to be baptized. Two and a half weeks later, he was baptized. We have seen him grow as a member of the Church, give

---

3. 1 Nephi 16:28; emphasis added.

his first talk, receive his first calling, and become an el-der in the Melchizedek Priesthood. He was a bit stressed and inexperienced, but he rose to meet all the standards with the help of the Lord.

Chapter 9

FAITH, HOPE, AND CHARITY

At least thirteen times in the scriptures there are statements that link together faith, hope, and charity. There seems to be a very important connection between these three Christlike attributes as they come together in power. In fact, the Lord has said that "if you have not faith, hope, and charity, you can do nothing."[1]

In the general sense, the term *faith* can be applied to almost any expectation we may have that something will happen, even though we haven't yet seen it. We have faith that the sun will rise tomorrow morning, or that the juice we drink will be nutritious, or that the brakes on the car will work when we step on the pedal.

The kind of faith the Lord is talking about, however, is a more profound and spiritual gift referred to as "faith in the Lord Jesus Christ."[2] This is a specialized kind of faith, a faith

---

1. Doctrine and Covenants 18:19.
2. Articles of Faith 1:4.

that is found in the gospel of Jesus Christ and, if cultivated and acted upon, will lead to salvation. You can enjoy the sunrise, care for your body, and trust in mechanics, but none of these will bring you any closer to heaven without a firm faith in our Savior.

Developing faith in Jesus Christ takes time and effort. It has to be coupled with hope, which we'll learn about in a moment, and must be based on truth. As Alma taught, "And now as I said concerning faith—faith is not to have a perfect knowledge of things; therefore if ye have faith ye hope for things which are not seen, which are true."[3]

Faith in Jesus Christ is the first principle of the gospel because everything else is based upon this foundational value. Without such faith, coupled with a confident reliance on the Atonement performed by the Lord, our ability to do His work is very limited. Your faith must include the belief that all the blessings of the Atonement apply to you *personally.* You have to believe that Jesus's suffering applies to you as well as to everyone else.

If you were to ask the people in your ward if they believe that Jesus died for our sins and was resurrected so we may all have eternal life, probably all would say yes. However, if you rephrased the question and asked if they have faith that the Atonement truly applies to them, you would probably get a few honest people who would say, "Not really." For some reason, we find it easy to have faith in the general application of the Atonement, but have a hard time believing that it can save someone like us. Our hearts are usually soft and tender for others, but sometimes hardened toward ourselves. (Remember

---

3. Alma 32:21.

that word *hardened*.) A story of Moses and Israel in the wilderness helps us understand this.

The ancient Israelites were a lot like us. At one point in their wandering in the wilderness, the people of Israel began to complain against Moses, their earthly leader, and the Lord Jehovah, their God.[4] It appears they became tired of searching for water in the desert and had lost their taste for manna, the breadlike substance the Lord had provided for them. In order to help them get back on track, the Lord sent poisonous serpents into their camp. What a stunning motivator! Many people were bitten and died, which humbled the people, helped them see their sinful ways, and brought them back to Moses, seeking his help in taking away the snakes. The dedicated prophet-leader Moses went to the Lord for the people and received divine instruction that would bring relief and teach them an important lesson at the same time.

Moses was commanded by the Lord to make a brass (brazen) serpent and put it on a pole for all to see. If the Israelites who were bitten would look upon the serpent, exercising their faith in the Lord, they would be healed. The Bible tells us this much of the story, but it doesn't offer any details or describe how things actually went in the camp of Israel.[5] We are blessed to have more information in the Book of Mormon.

Alma, in his preaching to the Zoramites, helps us understand that the brass serpent was meant to represent the Christ who would be lifted up on the cross and would serve as a source of healing for the people.[6] Alma explains that there were many

---

4. See Numbers 21:4–9.
5. See Numbers 21:4–9.
6. See Alma 33:19–20.

people in the camp of Israel who were bitten, looked upon the brass serpent, and were healed. There were many, however, who would not look upon the brass serpent even though their lives depended on it. Alma says they refused to do so because their hearts were hardened (remember that word?) and they did not believe that it would heal them.

In order to understand this, we have to read the scripture correctly. It says, "Now the reason they would not look is because they did not believe that it would heal them." Of course, they believed that it could heal others, because "many did look and live." The news of these healings must have spread like wildfire through the camp. Those who were healed would surely have advertised their joy and relief to all who would listen. Desperate people, dying of poisonous snakebite, would have been crazy not to seek whatever cure was available. Why then would some not take advantage of the sure cure? To find out, reread the passage and put the emphasis on the very last word. "Now the reason they would not look is because they did not believe that it would heal *them.*" They knew that healing could occur, they had seen it happen to others, but they didn't believe that it would work for *them*! Their hearts were hardened toward themselves, and they could not accept the healing blessing offered to all by the Lord. Sadly, their faith in the Lord's power to heal did not include themselves. True faith is complete trust in the universal power of Jesus.

That brings us to the wonderful principle of hope. To have hope is not just a matter of wishful thinking—not a casual, "Well, I hope so." Gospel-centered hope is a powerful belief in the Lord Jesus Christ and a faithful confidence that the Atonement has meaning *for you.* If you have hope in Jesus Christ, you will let your faith in Him rest peacefully and gently upon your own head and rejoice in the grace and mercy of the Lord as they are brought to pass in your own life.

When we have hope, we are motivated to keep the commandments. Hope based on faith in Jesus helps us be steady and consistent in our obedience. "Wherefore, whoso believeth in God might with surety hope for a better world, yea, even a place at the right hand of God, which hope cometh of faith, maketh an anchor to the souls of men, which would make them sure and steadfast, always abounding in good works, being led to glorify God."[7] Hopeful people are happy and confident that they will learn and grow and get better and better. They do good things and glorify God in the process.

So, you can see how faith and hope are connected. Faith in the Lord is based on the universal nature of the Atonement. Hope personalizes that faith and brings the Atonement into our individual lives. As Mormon wrote, "Wherefore, if a man have faith he must needs have hope; for without faith there cannot be any hope."[8] Now let's see how charity is connected.

Charity is defined beautifully as "the pure love of Christ."[9] Charity is not just love, it is the kind of love possessed by the Savior—pure, divine, selfless, and freely offered to others through compassionate service. This definition of charity far exceeds the kind but limited act of simply giving to those in need. It is significantly more than that. Charity is a powerful spiritual gift. We should seek it, but it is a blessing that comes to us only when we are worthy and prepared to receive it.

One way to look at the whole concept of charity is to divide

---

7. Ether 12:4.

8. Moroni 7:42.

9. Moroni 7:47.

it up into three elements: first, how we make ourselves worthy to receive this great gift; second, the way the Lord provides the gift; and third, how we act once the gift of charity is ours.

One of the great statements on charity is made by the Apostle Paul in the thirteenth chapter of First Corinthians. He speaks of great acts of righteousness, and says that these are mostly worthless if they are not done with charity. Paul goes on to list many of the qualities of someone who is worthy of the gift of charity. The list includes being patient, kind, humble, courteous, unselfish, slow to anger, and sincere, among other fine qualities. As we practice and develop these Christlike attributes, we will become more worthy and the spiritual gift of charity will develop in our lives. Of course, it is not expected that we be perfect from the beginning. Even though "the Lord cannot look upon sin with the least degree of allowance,"[10] in His tender mercy, He will bless us as we grow and keep trying to do what is right.

In another of his letters, Paul illustrates that as we "depart from iniquity," we will become more useful to the Master and better prepared for His work. He compares us to vessels (household containers) in a "great house." Some of the vessels are made of clay, some of wood, some of silver, and some of gold. The more pure the vessel, with gold being the most pure, the more honor is brought to the Master.[11] Our task is to become a golden vessel—a worthy and valuable servant of the Lord.

One of the biggest obstacles to becoming a golden vessel is the immaturity of youth. Paul counsels us to let go of our

10. Alma 45:16.
11. See 2 Timothy 2:19–21.

childish desires, to "follow righteousness, faith, charity, [and] peace, with them that call on the Lord out of a pure heart."[12] Missionaries have to grow up fast and "put away childish things."[13] In order to receive the most valuable spiritual gifts (and Paul says charity is among the greatest),[14] we must do our best to refine ourselves, rid ourselves of impurity, and become useful vessels (servants) of the Lord.

As we become more worthy vessels, the Lord will begin to fill us with His love.[15] That is another element in the development of the spiritual gift of charity. We will begin to feel love for those around us like we have never felt it before. It might begin with our family members and good friends, but as charity blossoms in our hearts, feelings of love will spread to people we don't even know. When you are a missionary, you will find that you really love the people of the area in which you are called to serve. That love may be felt even before you arrive in your mission area, and it will keep you going even when the work is hard. Every night as you're falling asleep and every morning when you wake up, you can let your love for the people give you peace and motivation for the coming day. When you are a worthy vessel, and your love for the Lord and His children begins to fill your very soul, you know you are receiving more of the gift of charity.

So, as the Lord fills His worthy servants with His love, their love deepens and grows into the kind of love we can call divine. This kind of love seems to come naturally to us when we seek

---

12. 2 Timothy 2:22.
13. 1 Corinthians 13:11.
14. See 1 Corinthians 13:13.
15. See Moroni 7:48.

it and are worthy of it. It feels right and brings great joy. As this love expands and fills us, it begins to overflow into the world around us in compassionate service. This is the third element of charity: compassion.

Frequently, in the four Gospels of the New Testament, reference is made to the Lord having compassion on those He met. (See, for example, Luke 7:11–15, where Jesus feels compassion for a widow and raises her son from the dead.) These feelings of compassion seem to come out of His pure love for the people. Deeds of compassion are love brought to action. If the love we feel is not acted upon in compassionate service to others, then our charity is not complete.

I love the missionary purpose statement in *Preach My Gospel.* It really describes what missionary work is all about. Missionaries are especially called to help people receive the restored gospel. The first part of the statement, however, refers to all of us: "Invite others to come unto Christ by helping them . . ."[16] Every act of compassion, just helping people, is an act of true charity. In compassionate service we emulate the Savior and, by our example, invite others to come to Him.

The three elements of charity are (1) being a worthy vessel, (2) allowing pure love to fill our souls, and (3) acting upon that love in compassionate service. This is a pretty simple formula, but it takes a lifetime and more to fully achieve.

Now, back to our doctrinal trio of faith, hope, and charity. Faith is our belief and trust in Jesus Christ and His Atonement. Hope is our confidence that the Atonement applies to us personally. Charity is being full of divine love and acting with

---

16. *Preach My Gospel: A Guide to Missionary Service* (2004), 1.

compassion and loving kindness toward ourselves and others. The three together form a perfect formula:

Jesus + Self + Others = peace and joy in this life and exaltation in the life to come.

"And now abideth faith, hope, charity, these three."[17] "And see that ye have faith, hope, and charity, and then ye will always abound in good works."[18]

In Their Own Words

The second day of my first week in a new city, my companion and I were doing our weekly planning. In order to give me a better understanding of who our investigators were, we were going through the area book and discussing each person. In doing so, we came upon the page of an old investigator from several years back. On the side margin of the back of his progress record was written the address and number of his apartment (#70) and his first name, Paul. I asked my companion if he knew who Paul was and he said no. We decided to take the address and go see if we could find him.

We quickly found the building, as it was right across from our bus stop. We entered the building and found a common eating area. There was one stairwell leading to four levels of single hallways. On the door into the first hallway was written "Doors 60–80." We pulled open the door, walked in, and surprised two people talking in the hallway. We excused ourselves and continued our search for door #70. Unfortunately, most of the doors

17. 1 Corinthians 13:13.
18. Alma 7:24.

were unmarked, so I turned around and said to the two people, "Excuse us, do you know which door is #70?"

An average-sized man, nicely dressed, with brief-case in hand, answered, "Yes, are you looking for Paul?"

"Yes," I replied, "do you know him?"

He said, "Well, yes. That's me! You are the mission-aries, right? I haven't seen one of you for about seven months. Come in. Let's talk for a little bit."

We had a strong first meeting with Paul. We shared a spiritual thought from Acts and invited him to be bap-tized. To our delight, he said yes! He has been to Church every week for three months and will soon be baptized. He is incredibly excited for his baptismal day and has been a great help for missionary work since day one. Many of his family and friends are being taught the re-stored gospel of Jesus Christ.

Chapter 10

JUST KEEP GOING

The sometimes tragic experiences of our early Church pioneers, though very difficult for them, can serve as an inspiration to us. Such is the case with the story of my third great-grandparents James and Sarah Ferguson McDonald.

James and Sarah were Irish immigrants who joined the Church and came to America in the late 1840s to join others of their faith and to have a better life for their family. From the beginning of their journey, they dreamed of making a new home among the Saints in the American West. In the spring of 1850, they started across the vast American plains as members of a large wagon train of pioneers with similar dreams.

Tragedy struck the family soon after they began. James contracted the dreaded disease cholera and died within twenty-four hours. He was buried in the trackless prairie on the banks of the Platte River. That evening, Sarah, in shock from the death of her beloved James, settled the children into their beds and then, with an aching heart and tired feet, went down to the river to wash off the dust of a terrible day. She took off her shoes and stockings and put her feet into the cool water.[1] Sarah could feel the strong current of the river, and in her grief she thought of how easy it would be to simply slide into the water, sink into the depths, and join her dear husband. But as she sat there, one of her young children called out to her, and she knew she had to carry on for them. She dried her feet, put on her shoes, and went back to the wagon. The next day, Sarah gathered her children and paused one last time at the grave of her husband. Then, looking west, she and her family walked on.

Sarah eventually established her family in a Rocky Mountain settlement. She lived a long and productive life, and her posterity now numbers in the thousands—all grateful for the faith, hope, and perseverance of their pioneer grandmother.

The courageous example of Sarah Ferguson McDonald and many, many others like her inspires us all, especially when our heart aches, our feet are tired, and we face a fearful future. Even then, we walk on.

When Ammon and his brethren were on their mission to the Lamanites, the going was very difficult. They had been warned by others that they would have no success among these people "whose hearts delight in the shedding of blood."[2] Understandably, these stalwart missionaries got a little depressed and wanted to go home. What a tragedy that would have been! So many good people would have missed the opportunity to hear the gospel message, and the spectacular missionary experiences of Ammon and his companions would never

---

1. See "Important Events in the History of the James McDonald Family, 1841–1850," Church History Library, Salt Lake City, Utah.
2. Alma 26:24.

have occurred. Thankfully, these missionaries were comforted by the Spirit of the Lord. They received the one word they needed to move them forward: "Go." Actually, it was a bit more than that. The Lord told them, "Go amongst thy brethren, the Lamanites, and bear with patience thine afflictions."[3] Loud and clear the Lord sent the message, "I never said it would be easy, I just told you to go! You will have hard times, but just go." But that wasn't all. He also gave them great confidence when He said, "I will give unto you success."[4] The missionary's responsibility is to go, to walk on. Success is the gift given by the Lord to those who keep going.

That doesn't mean it got any easier for Ammon and his fellow missionaries. Ammon describes how things went: "And now behold, we have come, and been forth amongst them; and we have been patient in our sufferings, and we have suffered every privation; yea, we have traveled from house to house, relying upon the mercies of the world—not upon the mercies of the world alone but upon the mercies of God. And we have entered into their houses and taught them, and we have taught them in their streets; yea, and we have taught them upon their hills; and we have also entered into their temples and their synagogues and taught them; and we have been cast out, and mocked, and spit upon, and smote upon our cheeks; and we have been stoned, and taken and bound with strong cords, and cast into prison; and through the power and wisdom of God we have been delivered again."[5]

In a very real way, that describes missionary work even

---

3. Alma 26:27.
4. Alma 26:27.
5. Alma 26:28–29.

today. You will go from house to house. You will teach people in their homes and in the streets, in parks and in churches, and sometimes you won't be very well received. There is probably no stoning or imprisonment in your future (though you wouldn't be the first!), but regardless, the Lord will deliver you.

One young missionary related to his mission president the story of how he and his companion were rudely rejected by someone. "It was great, President," he said. "We were persecuted just like the prophets of old!" Now, we don't hope for persecution or seek it out, but if it comes, we walk on. In the end, we will say with Ammon, "Now behold, we can look forth and see the fruits of our labors; and are they few? I say unto you, Nay, they are many."[6]

Great missionaries don't quit, even when the work is hard. (After all, it is called missionary *work*!) They don't let discouragement keep them down. Discouragement that is allowed to grow can result in feelings of helplessness and hopelessness. Discouragement is the fertile ground where temptation can take root until missionaries make mistakes that harm themselves and others. When things get hard, get up, forget about yourself, and keep going. If you do this, your discouragement will pass quickly.

If you keep going, follow the guidance of the Holy Ghost and of your leaders, and remain faithful, the Lord will give you success. Your success may not be measured in numbers, but you will see it and you will feel it. The fruits of your mission will be plentiful. Just remember to "walk on."

---

6. Alma 26:31.

In Their Own Words

My companion and I strove to be obedient. Out of respect toward other faiths we would not proselyte in front of other places of worship. We were walking down a busy street, speaking with those who passed by, and we made our way to the front of a beautiful cathedral. We slowly walked by, maintaining our respect for their beliefs, when we found ourselves being approached by a man. He was old and frail. He walked with a crutch and had broken glasses, messy hair, and a bag of clothes. He looked me in the eyes and said, "I was once like you."

The man once was a member of the Church. It had been over ten years since he had any sort of contact with anyone in the Church. He had lost everything. His family, his friends, his home, his free agency, and his relationship with the Savior. He was all alone. He was fighting for his life from alcohol poisoning. The next time we would see him would be months later in his hospital room.

Before our visit with him in the hospital, he had sent us a random text message asking that we contact the bishopric on his behalf. I remember him crying in the hospital. He told us he was going to end his life. The window from his lonely hospital room wasn't secure, and he knew what he was going to do. As he lay in bed, it was almost like a clock was ticking down the final minutes of his life. The man had absolutely nothing. He had no one. He had nothing to live for. He was hopeless. Just as time was running out, a quiet impression filled his mind: "Contact the elders." It was at that moment that he sent us a text message.

WHAT TO KNOW BEFORE YOU GO

We watched a man who was at the brink of death come back to life. While his addictions had robbed him, somebody remained mindful of him. His Savior saw potential. His Savior did not desert him. His Savior gave him a second chance. At that moment I realized that I had not only been called on a mission to teach. I had been called to be an instrument in saving lives.

Chapter 11

WHO WE
ARE MEANT TO BE

Nearly all children have dreams of what they would like to be when they grow up. Whether it is a fireman, a doctor, a pilot, or a princess, children have dreams. For some, their dream is to be like one of their heroes. When children—or adults, for that matter—read the Book of Mormon, many want to be like Nephi, son of Lehi, a hero of that sacred text. And what a hero he was, as he did with great faith everything that was asked of him.

Early on in the Book of Mormon, Nephi gives us some clues into his character. By paying attention to these and applying them in our own lives, we can become more like Nephi.

The first thing Nephi says about himself, besides the fact that he was young and very big for his age, is that he had "great desires to know of the mysteries of God."[1] He wanted to understand the gospel and gain some of the same knowledge that his father had. Mysteries are not necessarily mysterious,

---

1. 1 Nephi 2:16.

but usually some hidden treasure of knowledge that the world doesn't know about. Because they don't know, it is truly a mystery to them. Nephi really desired to know about these things of God.

Next, Nephi tells us what he did about it. He says, "I did cry unto the Lord."[2] This means he was raising his voice in prayer, seeking the blessing, guidance, and inspiration of the Lord. When we want to know something or be something, desiring is good, but seeking is vital.

Nephi was greatly blessed as the Lord spoke to his heart and he began to believe. That was the next step in his development. He went from desiring to seeking to believing. The words of his father and the revelation that came from the Lord went from his head to his heart and truly became a part of him. That is the process involved in gaining a testimony and becoming a believer.

Now that Nephi had a testimony of his own, he knew how he was supposed to act. He says, "I did not rebel . . . like . . . my brothers."[3] Nephi was obedient to his father's commands and to the commandments of God. He obeyed with exactness and did what he was supposed to do.

Some people complain about the Latter-day Saints and say we are like sheep, blindly obedient. As President Boyd K. Packer said, "We are not obedient because we are blind, we are obedient because we can see."[4] With the guidance of the Lord, Nephi could plainly see how to obey.

If you want to be like Nephi or any of the men and women

---

2. 1 Nephi 2:16.
3. 1 Nephi 2:16.
4. "Agency and Control," *Ensign*, May 1983, 66.

of God who have become our spiritual heroes, then follow the example of Nephi—desire, seek, believe, and obey. Nephi was young, some of his family members made life hard for him, he had to leave his comfortable home, and he had little idea what the future held in store for him, but he faithfully went forward with "lowliness of heart"[5] (humility), and he was prospered by the Lord. This will work for you, too.

In Their Own Words

My companion and I had planned to do street contacting when all of a sudden we had the strong feeling that we should start knocking on doors. We started to go from door to door, and everyone was rejecting us. We thought about Alma 5, which says that it is the humble who will accept the gospel. We were working in a well-to-do area, so we started walking and found a large building of humble apartments. We felt very strongly that this was where we should go.

Several doors were closed to us, but we kept trying until a door was answered by a small woman who looked very ill. She had the look of someone very sad and lonely. After a few minutes of talking, my companion said, "I think you need a blessing and my companion will give it to you." We entered her apartment and gave her a blessing. I can't tell you the words that were spoken, but she began crying and explained, "I now know with certainty that you were sent by God. This morning I prayed, asking God to guide me and help me, and you

---

5. 1 Nephi 2:19.

came. I just had a confirmation of that! I want to know everything!"

We taught this lady and she was baptized. She continues to this day in the joy of the gospel.

Chapter 12

A.S.K.:
ASK, SEEK, KNOCK

Often, the servants of the Lord have to go about their duty without knowing exactly where they are going to end up. The Spirit of the Lord will occasionally put us on the path of service without revealing in advance what the result will be. We just go forward with faith, ignoring our fears and trusting that the Lord will direct our path.[1] Nephi experienced this when he went back to Jerusalem to retrieve the brass plates. He "was led by the Spirit, not knowing beforehand the things which [he] should do."[2] That whole Jerusalem trip was difficult from the beginning, but Nephi knew the Lord would "prepare a way"[3] so he could accomplish what he was commanded to do.

Sometimes, only when we have fulfilled the purposes of the Lord can we look back, connect the dots, and see the reasons

---

1. See Proverbs 3:5–6.
2. 1 Nephi 4:6.
3. 1 Nephi 3:7.

why we did what we did. Usually, however, the Lord in His mercy will reveal to us early on what we need to do in our efforts to accomplish His will. He has given us a simple formula for discovering the way we should go. It is captured in three little words—**A**sk, **S**eek, and **K**nock—easily remembered with the acronym **A.S.K.**

At first glance, these three may appear to be the same thing—as if in one action we ask, seek, and knock, and thus get the direction we need. Upon closer consideration, however, we can see that these are three separate acts, each needing to be done before the answers will come and the Lord will give us the help we desire. Let's look at each one separately.

Missionaries need to know *what* the Lord would have them do. They need to ask Him for guidance regarding their activities. That is an essential element of the spiritual planning process in the everyday lives of full-time missionaries. How can anyone be sure they are on the right track if they don't have a conviction that what they are doing is correct? Imagine two missionaries kneeling together in their apartment, pleading with the Lord to know what they should do that day or the next. If they do so with faith, the Spirit will tell them as He speaks to their minds and hearts. They understand the promise that "Whatsoever thing ye shall ask in faith, believing that ye shall receive in the name of Christ, ye shall receive it."[4] These two young disciples of Christ won't stop asking until they know what the Lord would have them do.

Once they know what to do, they will want to know *how* to do it. That's where seeking comes in. Oliver Cowdery was chastised because, said the Lord, "You have not understood;

---

4. Enos 1:15.

you have supposed that I would give it unto you, when you took no thought save it was to ask me. But, behold, I say unto you, that you must study it out in your mind; then you must ask me if it be right."[5] The Lord expects us to do all we can to determine His will and to figure out how to accomplish it. If we ask, the Lord will tell us what we should do, but then we must "study it out" and seek His guidance to know how we should go about it.

The missionaries may receive the impression that they should contact people in a certain area, or visit a certain inactive member, or call a particular investigator. That is the what-should-we-do part of their spiritual planning. Once they know that, they talk together and seek the Spirit to decide how they can accomplish this task. If contacting is what they should do, how should they go about it? Should they be looking for a certain type of individual, or sharing a special message? If they are prompted to do some other task, they might ask, "How should we teach the member who may be struggling with her testimony?" or "How should we approach the investigator who is not keeping his commitments?" As they listen to the impressions of the Spirit, they will learn how to proceed.

The Lord promised, "For he that diligently seeketh shall find; and the mysteries of God shall be unfolded unto them, by the power of the Holy Ghost, as well in these times as in times of old, and as well in times of old as in times to come; wherefore, the course of the Lord is one eternal round."[6] This has been the Lord's way of guiding His servants from the very beginning, and it will likely always be.

---

5. Doctrine and Covenants 9:7–8.
6. 1 Nephi 10:19.

Once the missionaries know what to do and how to do it, they can, with faith and confidence, call upon the Lord for His help. It is written, "And whoso knocketh, to him will he open."[7] It's as if the Lord is standing at the door, ready and willing to help if we will just knock and request His assistance, but He *does* require that we knock. Consider the Lord's admonition, "Ask, and it shall be given you; seek, and ye shall find; knock, and it shall be opened unto you: For every one that asketh receiveth; and he that seeketh findeth; and to him that knocketh it shall be opened."[8] So far, so good, but let's see what might happen if we recast the second sentence as its opposite: "For every one that asketh [not] receiveth [not]; and he that seeketh [not] findeth [not]; and to him that knocketh [not] it shall [not] be opened." If we want the blessing, we have to do it the Lord's way, for "I, the Lord, am bound when ye do what I say; but when ye do not what I say, ye have no promise."[9]

The Lord has promised the missionaries they will have His guidance if they ask what, seek how, and knock for assistance. If they don't do their spiritual planning, but just hope for the best and wait to see what happens, they have no promise.

Before Jacob went to teach, he sought to obtain his "errand from the Lord."[10] He did his spiritual planning. This is essential for full-time missionaries, who are agents or representatives of the Lord. "Wherefore, as ye are agents, ye are on the Lord's

---

7. 2 Nephi 9:42.
8. Matthew 7:7–8.
9. Doctrine and Covenants 82:10.
10. Jacob 1:17.

errand; and whatever ye do according to the will of the Lord is the Lord's business."[11] In other words, if we don't ask and seek the Lord's will, we are telling Him that what we do is none of His business!

You can start now to develop your skill at spiritual planning. Think about having a humble and willing heart, being determined to do the Lord's business, to be His agent, and to be on His errand. Practice asking what, seeking how, and knocking so the Lord will open the door and be with you. Remember, **A.S.K.**

In Their Own Words

As my companion and I were contacting in a park near our apartment, we were not seeing a whole lot of success. As we were going to another area, my companion decided to go say hello to a Chinese man sitting on a bench nearby. We said hello and tried to talk to him in French, but he did not understand a thing we said. Then we gave English a try, and that didn't work either. After pointing to our name tags and trying to describe who we were by talking really, really slowly, we finally called the Chinese-speaking elders and handed the man the phone. As he talked to the other missionaries in Chinese, he sounded really excited. He even pulled out his little notebook to give them his telephone number. When he gave us the phone back, we found out that he had set up a meeting with them for the next week. After a few weeks of teaching, he was baptized. It was not only a

---

11. Doctrine and Covenants 64:29.

testimony to me that the Lord has people prepared to receive His truth, but also that the Spirit works through us missionaries. Even if we don't speak the same language, the Spirit speaks a universal language.

Chapter 13

LOVE YOUR COMPANION

One of the best things about full-time missionary service is being 24/7 with a companion. Your first companion, your trainer, will be handpicked by your mission president. With a great deal of prayer, consideration of your background and personality, and inspiration from the Lord, your mission president will look closely at all the eligible missionaries and choose the one he feels will give you the best possible start as a new missionary.

Each of your companions will bring different skills and experience to the mix. You will learn a great deal from each one. Sometime during your mission, the Lord and your mission president may trust you enough to send you a companion who needs your special attention. If this happens, consider yourself blessed, and do all you can to love and help your companion.

Generally, we love the best those we serve the most. Besides the vital rule to never leave your companion, there is the very important practice of serving your companion with love. We used to ask the missionaries to look at their shoes. If they were dirty or needed shining, the response would be, "Shame on your companion!" A loving missionary shines his companion's shoes, makes his bed, and does his dishes whenever the opportunity arises. A happy missionary will include her companion in every decision about the work, or even little things, like what they have for dinner or what they do on preparation day. If both of you are trying to serve each other, think of all the service that will take place! And you will be the recipient of much of it.

Get over using the word "I." Missionaries never do anything alone. Always include your companion by saying, "We." If someone asks you a question about the work or almost anything else you are doing as a missionary, respond with the first-person plural. Besides your family, to this point in your life you have probably never been as plural with anyone as you will be with your missionary companions.

Our family motto comes from an old Latin saying that, translated into English, says, "In essentials unity; in nonessentials liberty; in all things charity." This is a great guide for happy relationships. In those things that are essential, like mission rules and God's commandments, we must be unified. There is little room for compromise on the essentials. You and your companions should be completely united on those.

As for the nonessentials, like how fast you walk, what kind of toothpaste you prefer, or whether you like green beans, you should allow others the same liberty to choose that you want for yourself. We are fond of saying about such things, "You can still go to the celestial kingdom if you . . ." If that statement fits as you consider the choices your companions make, even if you disagree or are bothered by them, let them exercise their liberty and love them anyway.

There will be many times in your life when compassionate

compromise will be important. We should be full of Christlike loving kindness in all our relationships. Of course, we want our companionships to be pleasant and successful. The chances of succeeding are greatly increased if we practice charity, for "Charity never faileth." If things go wrong, fall back on the guidance the Lord has given us to use in building or rebuilding relationships. He has said:

"No power or influence [or companionship!] can or ought to be maintained by virtue of the priesthood, only by persuasion, by long-suffering, by gentleness and meekness, and by love unfeigned;

"By kindness, and pure knowledge, which shall greatly enlarge the soul without hypocrisy, and without guile—

"Reproving betimes with sharpness, when moved upon by the Holy Ghost; and then showing forth afterwards an increase of love toward him whom thou hast reproved, lest he esteem thee to be his enemy;

"That he may know that thy faithfulness is stronger than the cords of death.

"Let thy bowels also be full of charity towards all men, and to the household of faith, and let virtue garnish thy thoughts unceasingly; then shall thy confidence wax strong in the presence of God; and the doctrine of the priesthood shall distil upon thy soul as the dews from heaven." This is, of course, perfect counsel from the Lord. Let me add a personal perspective to the verse about "reproving betimes with sharpness."

The dictionary definition of *reprove* says that it means to reprimand or censure—in other words, to really get after somebody for doing something wrong. *Betimes* means early or in a timely manner. *Sharpness* means just that, in a sharp and maybe cutting way. So, the usual interpretation of "reproving betimes with sharpness" is reprimanding early in a cutting way. Ouch! You would really have to be moved upon by the Spirit to be justified in doing that.

Another way of interpreting those words would be "reproving or proving again, early and often, in a sharp or clear way." If your companion needs correction, rather than reprimanding him or her, you might accomplish a great deal more by proving again that you love your companion, doing it early and often, and being very clear in your expressions of love. That way of looking at it seems to fit well with the rest of the Lord's counsel in developing relationships.

I admit that I had a few missionary companions who tried my patience a little and didn't see things exactly as I saw them. That's what happens when two human beings spend a lot of time together. I did have a companion or two whom I wouldn't necessarily want to go on vacation with, but I loved each one and learned from them all.

Look for the good in your companions. They are probably just as worthy to be there as you are and are just as anxious to be successful, get along, and be happy. Seek the guidance of your leaders if needed, but be willing to do all you can to make your apartment a place where the Holy Ghost will want to dwell—a haven of unity, joy, and love.

In Their Own Words

Marie had been investigating the Church for about four years by the time we had the opportunity to teach her, and I must admit that I had my doubts concerning her. After pondering and praying every week about what we could teach her, it seemed like nothing we taught was getting through to her. We knew that she knew the gospel was true, so we extended the invitation of baptism at each visit. At each request, she would seize up in an emotional panic of reasons as to why she just couldn't accept—namely her husband, who disapproved of her visits with missionaries. We became quite disheartened and figured that it was her destiny to be an eternal investigator, and it was our fate to fail at showing her something she already knew to be true. It was a frustrating combination of emotions.

Amidst our visits to Marie, we had a missionary training meeting with the mission president where we were introduced to the new curriculum to be implemented throughout the missions of the world. As we discussed the need for investigators to receive revelation through the Book of Mormon, prayer, and Church attendance, my companion and I were filled with inspiration. We knew that our investigators needed to be receiving their own revelation, and we were determined to find out if ours had. We knew what we needed to do with Marie.

We scheduled an appointment with Marie right when we returned to our city. We saw her within the week and asked her very basic questions: "Can you explain what praying is like for you? What have your experiences at Church been like over the past few years? Do you feel the Spirit there?" These questions reminded us of many spiritual experiences she had had over her years as an investigator. Finally we asked the question, "Can you tell us your feelings about the Book of Mormon?" She mentioned that she had read it four times and that she loved the stories, but my companion and I understood something very quickly. She hadn't shared any revelatory experiences from the Book of Mormon. We felt inspired to read along with her at this point, so we began in 1 Nephi 1. We had her read the first verse: "I, Nephi, having been born of goodly parents . . ." At this point I stopped her. I then asked, "Tell me about your mother." Knowing beforehand about her family experiences and her deep love for her mother, the inspiration to ask that question came all at once. Tears began to stream down her face as she spoke about her mother and how she had been at her side at her passing. After sharing her experience, she said, "I have read this book four times and I have never understood what you missionaries meant by applying myself in the scriptures—until today." Tears filled our eyes as we extended the invitation to baptism once more, and she willingly accepted. She was baptized a few weeks later and is now the Relief Society president in her branch.

Chapter 14

WHEN YOU'RE AT YOUR WITS' END

When someone is stressed to the breaking point, with no idea of what to do next, we say they are "at their wits' end." There may be some times during your mission when you feel this way. You won't be the first of the Lord's disciples to have that happen, and hopefully you will find there is purpose in it, as did the early Apostles.

During the Savior's earthly ministry, He sometimes went from place to place by ship. On one such occasion, He and the disciples were sailing along when "there arose a great storm of wind, and the waves beat into the ship, so that it was now full [of water]."[1] As the storm raged, the Savior was in the back of the ship, apparently sound asleep. The disciples (several of whom were professional fishermen), seeing their desperate situation and fearing the ship would sink, awakened Jesus and said, "Master, carest thou not that we perish?"[2] The Lord then

1. Mark 4:37.
2. Mark 4:38.

"arose, and rebuked the wind, and said unto the sea, Peace, be still. And the wind ceased, and there was a great calm."[3]

The disciples were amazed by this. They could not believe that someone could have such power over the elements. Jesus questioned their fear and asked why they didn't have more faith, but the disciples "feared exceedingly, and said one to another, What manner of man is this, that even the wind and the sea obey him?"[4]

We know, of course, that Jesus was far more than just a man. He was and is the literal Creator of heaven and earth, and perfectly able to control His creations. We can probably know, also, that He was not just sleeping in the back of the boat. In fact, an early prophecy of this event is quite revealing.

A thousand years or so before Christ, people referred to as psalmists wrote inspired songs, many of which spoke about future events that related to the life of the Savior. One of these songs very clearly speaks of the fishermen, the ship, the wind and the waves, the fear of the sailors, and the Lord's calming of the storm.

"They that go down to the sea in ships, that do business in great waters;

"These see the works of the Lord, and his wonders in the deep.

"For he commandeth, and raiseth the stormy wind, which lifteth up the waves thereof.

"They mount up to the heaven, they go down again to the depths: their soul is melted because of trouble.

---

3. Mark 4:39.
4. Mark 4:41.

"They reel to and fro, and stagger like a drunken man, and are at their wits' end.

"Then they cry unto the Lord in their trouble, and he bringeth them out of their distresses.

"He maketh the storm a calm, so that the waves thereof are still.

"Then are they glad because they be quiet; so he bringeth them unto their desired haven."[5]

Isn't it amazing that the inspired psalmist could describe so exactly the future experience of the early Apostles? I love the tender description, "their soul is melted because of trouble." It is also very interesting that he says, "he [Jesus] commandeth, and raiseth the stormy wind." It seems the Lord was not asleep at all, but it was He who commanded and brought the storm to rock the boat. It was He who caused the big waves to come and fill the boat with water, which frightened these experienced sailors and finally brought them to "their wits' end."

You can just imagine Jesus in the back of the boat, perhaps dozing a bit, but fully aware of what was going on. He would have watched as the Apostles struggled to keep the ship afloat, the sails whipping in the wind and waves crashing on the deck. Only when the Apostles came to Him for help did He finally rise to their aid and, in a few words, bring peace and calm to the wind and water, as well as to the hearts of the fishermen.

By putting the two accounts together, from both Psalms and Matthew, we can understand what the Lord was trying to teach these newly called priesthood leaders. He may have said, "Don't be afraid when things are hard and frightening. I am here. Have faith. Call on Me and I will bring calm to

---

5. Psalm 107:23–30.

the situation. I will bring peace to your soul and guide you to where you need to be."

As a missionary, and at many other times in your life, you may well feel like you're at your wits' end. You will be driven to your knees in desperate supplication to Heavenly Father. You may cry out, "Father, I can't take this anymore. I'm going down! Please save me!" When that happens, remember He is not asleep. "Behold, he that keepeth Israel shall neither slumber nor sleep."[6] Even when you wonder where He is, you can trust that He and His angels are watching over you. Said He, "I will be on your right hand and on your left, and my Spirit shall be in your hearts, and mine angels round about you, to bear you up."[7]

The Lord will likely wait until you have learned from your trouble all He intended you to learn, until your soul is melted, and you are at the end of your rope. Even then, He may whisper, "Just tie a knot and hang on!" Before all is lost, however, you can trust that He will calm the storm and you will be safe. "Therefore, fear not, little flock; do good; let earth and hell [or wind and wave, or weariness, or confusion] combine against you, for if ye are built upon my rock [Jesus Christ], they cannot prevail."[8] Hang on. Keep doing the best you can. The calm will come.

In Their Own Words

Contacting less-active members can be very rewarding, but also very frustrating. My companion and I

---

6. Psalm 121:4.
7. Doctrine and Covenants 84:88.
8. Doctrine and Covenants 6:34.

went to visit Charles, a man who had not been to Church in over seven years. He invited us into his home, but then spent over an hour just "bashing" with us. He told us we were hypocrites and we should take off our name tags and go home.

At one point, for some reason I asked him, "Have you been reading the Book of Mormon?" Of course, he had not. We shared a brief message from the book of Mosiah (Mosiah 4:9–10) and talked about believing. None of this seemed to make much of an impression on him.

Two weeks later we decided to go and see Charles again. He was a changed man. He told us that he had started to read the Book of Mormon and was up to Mosiah. We asked him how he felt about what he was reading. We were so happy when he began crying and told us he knew it was true.

Chapter 15

TESTIMONY

The goal of every missionary companionship is to help their investigators receive a testimony of the restored gospel of Jesus Christ. You will be given all the tools you need to assist in this process, particularly the Holy Ghost and the holy scriptures. As it says in *Preach My Gospel,* "The Book of Mormon, combined with the Spirit, is your most powerful resource in conversion."[1] Almost nothing builds testimony like the powerful combination of the Book of Mormon and the witness of the Holy Ghost.

Still vivid in my memory is the moment when I received a sure witness of the truth of the Book of Mormon. As a young man, I was reading this sacred work with "real intent"[2] for the first time, and the Spirit really spoke to my mind and my heart[3] to give me a testimony of the Book of Mormon and the calling of the Prophet Joseph Smith. In my mind I knew

---

1. *Preach My Gospel: A Guide to Missionary Service* (2004), 104.
2. Moroni 10:4.
3. See Doctrine and Covenants 8:2.

the book was true, and in my heart I felt the witness. In this way, my testimony was born and has been reborn many times. I can say, "I know that the gospel of Jesus Christ, as restored through the Prophet Joseph, is true. I know that The Church of Jesus Christ of Latter-day Saints is the only true and living church upon the earth today." But I didn't gain that knowledge all at once. It has come gradually and with a great deal of effort.

For a small number of people, the creation of a testimony comes in a rather dramatic way. For a few, angels have appeared, visions have been seen, and voices have been heard from heaven. For most of us, a testimony comes "precept [or principle] upon precept; line upon line, line upon line; here a little, and there a little,"⁴ as we grow in conviction and confidence that we really know. What a joy it is to bear testimony to others and feel the Spirit bear witness to you at the same time. The more you speak your testimony, the stronger it will become.

It is extremely important to remember that gaining a testimony does not guarantee you will keep it. So many sad and sometimes angry people claim to have "lost" their testimony. They didn't just lose it, they let it die. Like any spiritual gift, a testimony has to be very carefully nurtured in order to be maintained. President Harold B. Lee, eleventh President of the Church, said, "Testimony isn't something you have today, and you are going to have always."⁵ He added, "Testimony is as

4. Isaiah 28:10.
5. *Church News,* July 15, 1972, 4.

85

elusive as a moonbeam; it's as fragile as an orchid; you have to recapture it every morning of your life. You have to hold on by study, and by faith, and by prayer."[6]

I can't imagine anything more elusive or hard to hold on to than a moonbeam! Thank heaven we can have the frequent whisperings of the Spirit to help us keep our testimony going and growing. We must also do our part through study, faith, and prayer. If we ask, seek, and knock (remember **A.S.K.**?) the Lord will bless us with the knowledge and assurance we desire.

If you don't think you have a firm testimony, or you feel like you can't say that you know, then trust in those who *do* know and would never try to deceive you. Until you have your own testimony, you can lean on your parents, priesthood leaders, and others who have received the witness. That will be a manifestation of your faith, and you will be blessed. Continue your study of the scriptures and keep praying for the knowledge you hope for. It will come when you are ready and the Lord, knowing your heart and seeing your desire, sends His blessing.

Remember Moroni's promise that if you "would ask God, the Eternal Father, in the name of Christ, if these things are not true; and if ye shall ask with a sincere heart, with real intent, having faith in Christ, he will manifest the truth of it unto you, by the power of the Holy Ghost."[7] If you really want to know, ask God! Don't ask those who don't believe and have come up with arguments that would convince you not to believe. Satan and his followers have deceived many with their half-truths

---

6. *Teachings of Presidents of the Church: Harold B. Lee* (2000), 43.
7. Moroni 10:4.

and outright lies. One sure way to weaken a testimony is to spend time reading the ramblings of those who tear down the truth but offer nothing of any value to replace it. They don't deserve your attention. To trust them causes confusion and can be deadly to your testimony.

As a missionary, every day you will have many opportunities to bear your testimony. As you do so, it will grow. Your conviction will sink deep into your heart and your conversion will be real and sure. If you take time to "recapture it every morning of your life," your testimony will bless your life forever.

In Their Own Words

One day we were passing back to some addresses of former investigators that we found in the area book. We knocked on some doors, but had no success. One address was particularly hard to find. We started turning corners and going down streets trying to find this place until, after a while, we were lost. We had no idea where we were, but my companion felt like we should keep going. Suddenly, we received a phone call from a man who was not active in the Church and was the only member of the Church in his family. He had looked out of his window right in time to see us walk by, so he invited us in. It turned out that he was in the process of making a big decision in his life and needed help from the Lord. We were able to give him and his nonmember son a blessing. We were there for him in his time of need, even though we had never met before. It was a very spiritual experience and a testimony to me that we are led by the Spirit. We just kept walking, even when we thought we were lost, and we were able to bring comfort and the Spirit to those in need. That's what being a missionary is all about. When we are working and trying our best, we can be instruments in the Lord's hands.

Chapter 16

SUCCESS

How many baptisms did you get?" Ah, the ultimate question. A reasonable question, perhaps, since you will go on your mission to baptize people, but certainly not the right measure of a successful mission.

Some missions, for a variety of reasons, receive more converts than others. In France, we used to say, "Every time we knock on a door in France, they baptize someone in Mexico!" Of course, that's not entirely true, and we had many wonderful converts in France, but people in some areas do seem to be more responsive to the gospel message. So, is a missionary in Mexico automatically more successful than one in France? Absolutely not!

What does make a missionary successful? *Preach My Gospel* makes it perfectly clear: "Your success as a missionary is measured primarily by your commitment."[1] Missionary success is determined by your commitment as demonstrated by your faith, obedience, and diligence (remember FOD?). I recall clearly being told as a young missionary by President Marion G.

---

1. *Preach My Gospel: A Guide to Missionary Service* (2004), 10.

Romney, who served in the First Presidency, that our success was not determined by the number of baptisms we had but by our diligence in speaking to as many people as possible and inviting them to come to Christ. Whether or not they accepted our invitation was up to them, not us. Their response did not determine our success.

Preach My Gospel even clarifies how we make that invitation. In describing the missionary purpose, it says you should "invite others to come unto Christ by helping them."[2] There are important details added to your purpose, but the bottom line is just that simple. If you spend your time helping people in such a way that you are inviting them to follow the Savior, you are being a successful missionary.

If you do want to focus on baptisms, then feel free to take some credit for every baptism that takes place in the mission. No one stands alone. You may find an investigator who is taught by other missionaries and baptized by still others. You may contact a person on the street who is too busy to listen but will remember you and your companion and be more willing to listen the next time he or she is contacted. In addition, the obedience of each missionary contributes to the overall culture, spirituality, and success of the entire mission. What you and your companion do in your little area has a great impact on the efforts of every missionary in your mission. When our missionaries were asked how many baptisms they had, we hoped they would respond, "Oh, about five hundred." When a team or a family has success, everyone can feel a part of it.

Two missionaries were walking down the street on their way to an appointment. A woman looked out her window and

2. *Preach My Gospel,* 1.

saw them. She said to herself, "I hope my two sons will grow up to be fine-looking men like these." Months later, two different missionaries knocked on her door. She remembered seeing the others and so invited these elders in to give their message. It often takes several contacts with the Church and its members before someone is ready to hear the message of the restored gospel.

A fine sister missionary and her companion contacted a woman on a bus in their assigned area in a city in France. She told them she was soon to leave on a trip to America and would not have time to see them before she left. The sisters bore their testimony, challenged the woman to look up the Church while in America, and then kind of forgot about her. Months later, after serving elsewhere, one of the sisters was reassigned to that same city, something that doesn't usually happen. On her first Sunday back, she was welcomed to Church meetings with smiles and a big hug from a member she didn't recognize. "You don't remember me, do you?" said the good woman with a twinkle in her eye. The missionary was puzzled. She thought she knew all the members of this small ward. The woman explained, "You met me on a bus over a year ago, just before I went to America. I met the missionaries there and remembered your testimony and your challenge. I was taught the gospel and have been baptized." What a great and satisfying success for these missionaries! You never know when your seed-planting efforts will bear abundant fruit.

One of the biggest roadblocks to feeling successful is comparing yourself with others. Comparing doesn't have much of an upside. When you judge yourself against someone else, if you come out on top you are likely to feel prideful—better than other people. If you judge yourself as less than others, you run the real risk of becoming discouraged. Pride will cloud your judgment and make it harder to feel the Spirit and serve others with compassion. Discouragement will slow you down, rob you of your love for others, cause you to be homesick, and take all the joy out of your missionary labors. Don't compare yourself to others. Just do all you can to strengthen your commitment to be faithful, obedient, and diligent, and you will have success.

When you go to the temple to receive your own endowment, you will gain greater understanding of the law of consecration. To consecrate is to devote all you have and all you are to the purposes of God on the earth. Those who strive to do this will not be forgotten by the Lord, even though they make mistakes along the way. His promise is that "inasmuch as ye are humble and faithful and call upon my name, behold, I will give you the victory."[3]

On May 13, 2005, Ed Viesturs (pronounced veesters) stood on the perpetually snowy summit of K-2, a towering Himalayan mountain peak. On what he described as one of the hardest but happiest days of his life, he completed a sixteen-year quest to climb all of the world's mountains that reach above 26,000 feet, including Mt. Everest. And he did it without the use of supplemental oxygen—a feat some deemed impossible! Preparation and perseverance saw him through extreme physical and emotional challenges and allowed him to realize his dream of climbing all fourteen of the highest mountains on earth. All this was born of Viesturs's almost superhuman commitment to his goal.[4]

---

3. Doctrine and Covenants 104:82.
4. See Ed Viesturs and David Roberts, *No Shortcuts to the Top* (2006).

This remarkable accomplishment is a vivid reminder that some goals take many years to complete. Works of enduring value are based on patient determination. It also demonstrates that efforts to do something important are realized one step at a time. With every trudging step up the mountain and every labored breath, Ed Viesturs was realizing the fruits of his commitment.

Unfortunately, sometimes even our most heartfelt resolutions go unfulfilled. Perhaps our goals are too high and exceed our actual ability to perform, or they may be unrealistic in some other way. Using good judgment and knowing our limits are essential in deciding what actions to pursue and how to go about doing them. With careful planning, patience, and persistence, we can establish and achieve worthy goals. Often, the guidance of people who care about us is essential in the process.

Like the mountain climber, we must carefully plan out a route to our chosen peak of achievement and then work our way to the summit by putting one foot in front of the other. In the end, if we continue in our commitment, we'll be rewarded with a gratifying view from the heights of our potential.

And should we become discouraged along the way, we can pause to catch our breath, refocus our resolve, and then push ahead. Goals are not fulfilled by luck, or destiny, or genetic endowments. Success comes through sincere commitment applied with wisdom and foresight.

As the poet Ella Wheeler Wilcox declared in her poem "Will":

> *There is no chance, no destiny, no fate,*
> *Can circumvent or hinder or control*

The firm resolve of a determined soul.
Gifts count for nothing; will alone is great;
All things give way before it, soon or late.
What obstacle can stay the mighty force
Of the sea-seeking river in its course,
Or cause the ascending orb of day to wait?
Each well-born soul must win what it deserves.
Let the fool prate of luck. The fortunate
Is he whose earnest purpose never swerves,
Whose slightest action or inaction serves
The one great aim. Why, even Death stands still,
And waits an hour sometimes for such a will.[5]

Look into your heart. Go to the Lord and offer up your whole soul to him. Your commitment to that offering and your resolve to be the best missionary you can be will see you through. If you are a hardworking missionary on the Lord's errand, regardless of your statistical achievements, He will look into your heart and call you a success.

In Their Own Words

One day we were out contacting people on the street. We met an African man and learned that his name was Thomas and he came from the country of Angola. Within a few minutes, he had a copy of the Book of Mormon in his hands, we had his phone number, and he accepted an invitation to come and watch general conference at the chapel on Sunday. On Friday, we gave Thomas a call to renew the invitation and he showed up to the priesthood session of conference. The next day he

---

5. In *Poetical Works of Ella Wheeler Wilcox* (1917), 129–30.

told us, "I love this. These men speak the truth. I'm really excited about this!"

By the time I was transferred from the city, Thomas had been taught almost all the lessons and was coming to church weekly. I was later able to return and witness the baptism of this faithful man. Thomas will be returning to his home country soon, but right now he is a teacher in the elders quorum in the ward and loving it. A few weeks ago, he wrote me an email saying, "I have tears in my eyes just thinking about what this gospel has done for me."

Chapter 17

HOW TO TEACH

If you grow up in the Church and regularly attend Sunday meetings and other classes and devotionals, you will receive more than 3,000 hours of instruction. That's a lot! It may be, however, that you were never asked to actually teach even one hour of lesson yourself. I don't recall ever teaching a formal lesson as a youth in the Church. What I do remember is teaching a lesson on practically the first day I arrived in the mission field. And that in a foreign language!

But don't worry! You will receive wonderful instruction and lots of teaching practice in the Missionary Training Center. *Preach My Gospel* is full of excellent teaching tools, and you will have a great senior companion-trainer to help and guide you in your first area. In addition, the Lord has given some special revelation to help you understand the teaching process for missionaries and other gospel instructors.

In 1833, Joseph Smith and Sidney Rigdon were sent to preach the gospel in New York. They were feeling some concern about home and, I suppose, about being good missionaries, so the Lord gave them assurance that "I, the Lord, have suffered [caused] you to come unto this place; for thus it was expedient [useful] in me for the salvation of souls."[1] The Lord will also direct where you are called to serve.

The Lord then gave these good missionaries some guidance in how they should teach. As recorded in the next several verses of this revelation, He instructed them to (1) "lift up your voices," (2) "speak the thoughts that I shall put into your hearts," (3) do it "in my name," (4) "in solemnity [seriousness] of heart," and (5) "in the spirit of meekness."[2] He then promised that "the Holy Ghost shall be shed forth in bearing record unto all things whatsoever ye shall say."[3] That is the perfect formula for successful gospel teaching.

First, you have to be willing to speak. Your shiny shoes and your bright smile are helpful, but your voice is really important in getting the message across to your investigators. You are the vessel that the Lord will use to bring His word to those who need it. You and your companions are the ones who have to speak up.

Next, you can trust that the Lord will put into your heart and mind the words that will be most helpful to the person you are teaching.

I love the story of Samuel the Lamanite, who went to the land of Zarahemla to teach the Nephites. He was thrown out of the land by the wicked people, but told by the Lord to return. The Lord promised that He would put into Samuel's heart the things he should say. So Samuel went back and "prophesied unto the people whatsoever things the Lord put into his

---

1. Doctrine and Covenants 100:4.
2. Doctrine and Covenants 100:5–7.
3. Doctrine and Covenants 100:8.

heart."[4] He bore testimony that "I, Samuel, a Lamanite, do speak the words of the Lord which he doth put into my heart; and behold he hath put it into my heart to say . . ."[5] The best teachers teach from the heart.

Your trust in this process will be greatly increased if you and your companion are prepared and worthy to receive the guidance of the Spirit of the Lord. In preparation, you must study the lesson material and "treasure up in your minds continually the words of life."[6] Pray about the individual needs of your investigators, and plan the best way to present the lesson in order to meet those needs. As you do this, "it shall be given you in the very hour, yea, in the very moment, what ye shall say."[7]

All the gospel teaching we attempt should be done in the name of Jesus Christ, for "all things must be done in the name of Christ, whatsoever you do in the Spirit."[8] As long as you are wearing that missionary badge, you are His official representative and have the right to speak in His name. Understanding and remembering this will give you solemnity of heart, and you will take very seriously your responsibility to teach.

The next instruction from the Lord is about meekness. To be meek is to be gentle and mild. Meek people are not easily offended and are quick to forgive. Meekness is not exactly the same as humility, but these two Christlike virtues are in the same family. When the Savior taught during His earthly ministry, He was always meek, even when He was bold and direct.

---

4. Helaman 13:4.
5. Helaman 13:5.
6. Doctrine and Covenants 84:85.
7. Doctrine and Covenants 100:6.
8. Doctrine and Covenants 46:31.

When you teach with meekness, you will avoid anger and contention, which are enemies of the Spirit.

In the end, real learning will not occur unless the Holy Ghost touches the heart of the one you are teaching and bears witness of the truth of your message. No missionary ever converted anyone. The Holy Ghost takes the message into the mind and heart of the one who listens and helps that person to know and feel the truth.

Teaching comes naturally to some. Others have to work harder at it, and some really struggle, but as you prepare to the best of your ability and trust in the Lord, miracles will occur. Words will come to you, the Holy Ghost will confirm your testimony, and you will see the wonderful conversion of people you have learned to love.

In Their Own Words

At one point, my companion and I started to run out of progressing investigators. We decided, during our weekly planning session, that we needed to be more specific about who we were looking for. We felt that we should search for a woman with a baby stroller who would be ready to receive the gospel. Within two days, we had found two women who were walking with baby strollers. One would be baptized with her family five weeks later. The other turned out to be a less-active member. She returned to Church after twenty years of inactivity. This tender mercy that God gave to us has enormously increased my faith in His work and has helped me through several difficult trials.

Chapter 18

POWER AND AUTHORITY

In the inspired dedicatory prayer for the Kirtland Temple, the Prophet Joseph Smith made special reference to the missionaries who would receive temple blessings before they left to serve:

"And we ask thee, Holy Father, that thy servants may go forth from this house armed with thy power, and that thy name may be upon them, and thy glory be round about them, and thine angels have charge over them;

"And from this place they may bear exceedingly great and glorious tidings, in truth, unto the ends of the earth, that they may know that this is thy work, and that thou hast put forth thy hand, to fulfil that which thou hast spoken by the mouths of the prophets, concerning the last days."[1]

As you go into the mission field, you will be endowed with the power of God to fulfill His purposes. You will be guided and directed by angels, unseen beings from beyond the veil, who are greatly interested in you. You will be set apart as an ordained minister, taking part in the final gathering of the elect

1. Doctrine and Covenants 109:22–23.

prior to the Second Coming of the Lord. What an incredible opportunity and awesome responsibility!

You may not feel good enough or smart enough to meet the challenge of missionary work. That's a normal feeling and a sign of appropriate humility. Rest assured you will do just fine. Many thousands have gone before you, many not as well equipped as you, and they have served with honor.

President Gordon B. Hinckley often met with missionaries during his ministry. He loved to tease them by saying, "You're not much, but you're all the Lord has." The Lord Himself was referring to men and women like you when he said, "The fulness of my gospel [will] be proclaimed by the weak and the simple unto the ends of the world, and before kings and rulers."[2] Even Jesus was considered weak and simple by His earthly enemies, but He possessed the power and authority of heaven. You will possess that same power as you labor under the priesthood keys of your mission president.

Never forget who you are and who you represent. Be that person twenty-four hours a day and seven days a week from the day you are set apart by your stake president until the day you are released. Even after that, stay true to your missionary ideals. I recall a fine elder who asked me at his final interview before going home, "President, what do I do now?" My response was, "Elder, just keep doing what you've been doing for the past two years and you'll be fine." In other words, remain faithful, read the scriptures every day, and take time to plan and pray.

One returned missionary took this advice literally. When he called to let me know he was engaged to be married, I asked him how he had found his future bride. "It was easy," he said.

---

2. Doctrine and Covenants 1:23.

"I just did what we used to do as missionaries. I used public transportation and looked for a seat next to someone who might be interested in me. I finally found a girl who was willing to learn more!"

When you are released, you will miss the authority to serve as a full-time missionary, but the power you gain in the process of your missionary service never needs to leave you. In fact, it would be very sad if it did. You will be empowered by your temple experience. You will be empowered by your experiences as a missionary. Your task for the rest of your life will be to build on that power and be the best husband and father or wife and mother you can be.

In Their Own Words

Shortly after receiving training from our district leader on our mission's Standards of Excellence, my companion and I decided to put our faith to the test and try with all our might, mind, and strength to teach twenty lessons in a single week. [Mission average was less than ten!] The week prior to the week when we planned to teach all these lessons, we tried our best to schedule as many appointments as possible. We did this by making a myriad of phone calls, passing by people's homes to make return appointments, and finding people on the streets who would be interested in meeting with us. We didn't want to teach twenty lessons for our own glory, but to show others and ourselves that it was possible, not to mention to help those we taught along the way.

On the first day of our week, we encountered many problems. There was a bus strike that reduced us to walking . . . everywhere. But, with our faith and hope, we did so. That first day, we ended up with only one lesson, though we had four planned at the beginning of the day. Things weren't looking very good to either of us, but we continued.

Every second of our time that week, it seemed, was focused on finding people to teach. By Friday night, we had thirteen lessons. On Saturday, we started seeing miracles. We were able to meet with five less-active families that day, and we did much good for each of them. The greatest thing of that day came when we went to visit a sister who we may not have visited if we had not been trying to stretch ourselves to these new limits. Upon arriving at her home, we met one of her friends who was just leaving. He became a serious investigator and was baptized one month later. We were led by Heavenly Father to be in the right place at the right time because we were working toward an important goal.

Back to our quest for twenty lessons. Sunday morning rolled around and we were sitting at a nice and comfortable eighteen lessons for the week. We had five appointments lined up for the day, so we thought we could easily make our goal. A new investigator came to church with a friend and we were able to teach him, so by 11:30 we had nineteen lessons. Our goal seemed like a sure thing, even when we learned that all but one of our appointments for the rest of the day had to be postponed. We still had that one appointment.

On Sunday evening, we walked three miles to our last appointment, knocked on the door, and nobody answered. We later learned that the man had been called away for a family emergency. So there we were, three miles from home with nineteen lessons for the week. Part of me felt satisfied, but another part didn't understand why we couldn't reach our goal after so much planning and hard work. We had prayed and Heavenly Father had endorsed our goal, but at that moment I doubted. Thankfully, my companion courageously said, "We're not giving up!"

I quickly said a personal prayer and asked for help. I knew what we were doing was the will of the Lord and that there was no reason for Him not to help us. We were, after all, about His business, not our own. We then set off to find someone who would allow us to share the gospel with them. We went door to door for an hour and a half with no success. Door after door was shut in our face. At this point it was getting late, and it was very difficult to continue any more. On the verge of giving up, we told ourselves, "Just a few more. We'll find somebody in just a few more tries."

Five doors later, a nice older lady answered. When she saw us, she said, "Wait here, I'll get my husband; he'll want to talk with you." We couldn't believe our ears! We were going to have our twentieth lesson! The man invited us in, and we learned that he had been an investigator some years before. He had read the Book of Mormon and prayed about it, but didn't feel that he had received an answer to his prayers. We testified of the love of God for all of His children and promised that He would respond to his prayers if they were earnest. We invited him to read the Book of Mormon again and to continue to pray. This began our teaching of a good man.

POWER AND AUTHORITY

My companion and I really put our faith to the test, and it paid off. Because we saw the fruits of our faith, our faith grew exponentially. Our mission president was inspired to tell us that twenty lessons per week was possible, we tried it, and it worked. Not only did it work, but one man was baptized and many others were taught the truths of the restored gospel. I learned that I really can put my trust in the Lord, even in the most dismal-looking circumstances.

Chapter 19

HITTING THE TARGET

O ne of the skills you will master as a missionary is the ability to set realistic goals. As you learn to do this, you will find great joy in exercising your faith and accomplishing more than you ever dreamed you could. An episode in my early life taught me a great lesson about how to achieve righteous goals.

As a young military officer, I wanted desperately to win a ribbon to pin in the empty space above the name tag on my uniform. It seemed like I was the only one on the base who didn't have a splash of color on his chest. Most had several ribbons, and a few had so many that they appeared a little slant-shouldered as they walked. They were loaded down with honor. All I had was a plastic name tag.

The day came when I had a chance to earn a ribbon, but my hopes were not too high. The training exercise was pistol shooting. Unfortunately, only those who hit the target with expert proficiency would win the right to wear the marksman ribbon.

I had shot a pistol only once before and couldn't hit the proverbial broad side of a barn. It seemed like every breath or blink of the eyes put my aim off just enough to make me miss the tin can or whatever target it was my intention to hit. My only chance to win this ribbon lay in listening carefully to the expert instructor, applying everything he suggested, and hoping for the best.

The first thing he taught us was how to hold the pistol so it would be steadier in our hands. "Good," I thought. "I can do that. It will help. Maybe I can hit the target!"

The next thing he said made very little sense and replaced my budding confidence with confusion. His statement went against every notion I had practiced as a child when it came to hitting something with a projectile of whatever kind, be it a snowball, a rock, or a ball. The instructor said, "If you can see the target, you won't hit it!"

I said to myself, "What? How am I supposed to hit it if I can't see it? What kind of an expert is this guy, anyhow? Well, he's the kind of expert who has a lot of ribbons on his chest, so maybe I'd better listen and figure out what he is trying to tell us."

The instructor went on to explain the obvious fact that our eyes can't focus on two separate objects at the same time if one of the objects is close and the other is distant. Try it! Try focusing on something right in front of you and, at the same time, on some object across the room. See, it really can't be done. You can kind of see both at once, but you can't *focus* on both at the same time. The sights of the pistol, when held at arm's length, were only a couple of feet from my eyes. The target, on the other hand, was some fifty feet or more away. It was impossible to focus on both at once.

It seemed natural to pay greatest attention to the object of my aim—the target. But if I focused my eyes on the target, then the sights of the gun were blurry and could not be aligned well enough to make a good shot. The pistol may be steady, I might have the target well in mind and know exactly what I want to hit, but if the sights are not properly focused, the shot will go awry. I'll miss the bull's-eye. No ribbon.

The solution to this dilemma was surprisingly simple. We young officers were instructed to first look forward down the barrel of the pistol and focus on the target. It is important to know what we want to hit, what we want to achieve. We have to know where the bull's-eye is!

When we felt comfortable with the target, then our eyes could be focused on the sights of the pistol, not far from the end of our nose. It was vital that the sights be clearly in focus and aligned just right when the gun discharged, sending the bullet toward the target.

In missionary work, we may be tempted to focus on the distant goal—baptisms—but neglect to take care of the steps that will take us there. Sometimes we think we know where we want to go, but we are unwilling or unable to line things up correctly so we will end up where we hope to be. Personal worthiness, spiritual planning, spiritual finding, and spiritual teaching—those are the steps that must be taken in order to finally hit the target of baptisms.

Every missionary wants to baptize, but not all seem interested in doing what it takes today to achieve the goal in what may seem like a distant tomorrow. Don't worry about baptisms. That can result in too much focus on the target and not enough attention paid to the tasks at hand. And if you can see the target, you won't hit it.

So, we must first get a vision of the target, understand our goal and what results we want for our effort. We must have a good understanding of the direction we want things to go.

Second, we should focus on that which is right in front of us. We must pay attention to the tasks within our immediate reach. They have to be done right. Then, when we pull the trigger, all the power will be pointed in the direction we want it to go.

When we pay close attention to the small things in life, the big things have a way of taking care of themselves. It works! In my very short military career, it was the only ribbon I won.

In Their Own Words

When my companion and I became the second team of missionaries in a ward, we focused on helping ward members become more involved in missionary work. One idea was to ask a family to help us know where to search for new investigators. We set up a meeting with a member of the bishopric and his family. During the meeting, we shared some scriptures, one of which was 1 Nephi 17:50–51, which says in part, "If God had commanded me to do all things I could do them. If he should command me that I should say unto this water, be thou earth, it should be earth; and if I should say it, it would be done. And now, if the Lord has such great power, and has wrought so many miracles among the children of men, how is it that he cannot instruct me, that I should build a ship?" Or reveal to us where someone is prepared to receive the gospel!

We invited the family to pray every day to know where in their area we should go to find someone to teach. The following week we returned to see what the family had learned. They told us that this had been a real trial of their faith and that they weren't sure it would work, but the father handed us a piece of paper with three street names on it. He explained that his ten-year-old daughter had gone into her room, prayed, and come out with the paper. He was a bit skeptical, but we took it seriously. In addition to the three street names, there was a specific description of a person. The paper said "a young single mom with two kids and is sad."

Later, we went to the area indicated on the paper. While we were walking to the street where we planned to start contacting, we noticed a lady who had pulled up in front of her house and was unloading stuff from her car. We stopped to talk with her and offered to help her. Upon finding out who we were, she asked if we could come in right then, because her two sons needed to hear our message.

Through the course of the lesson, we found out that her husband had passed away a few months prior and, because of that and other things, she was having a lot of sadness in her life. She fit perfectly the description given to us by the ten-year-old girl.

Over time, we were able to see this woman transform from a life of sadness and misery to a life full of understanding, joy, and happiness. This was a powerful witness of the healing power of the gospel and of the faith of a ten-year-old girl.

Chapter 20

BECOMING WHO YOU ARE

I spoke with someone recently who had just left her teens and was entering into young adulthood and preparing for missionary service. I gave her advice and tried to create some images to which she could relate so she could develop a sense of what this new stage of her life was all about—responsibility, stability, learning, work, formalizing her preparation for life. Neither one of us thought it sounded like she was in for much fun. Thank heaven it sounds worse than it is!

As our conversation came to an end, I asked if she understood what I was trying to tell her. She said she did, but then posed the best question possible after such a talk: "But how do you do it?"

Excellent question! How do we implement all the good things we learn? How do we act in line with what we know?

I was sitting in sacrament meeting one day when an interesting thought came to mind. When Jesus was being crucified, He made a remarkable request of Heavenly Father. "Then said

Jesus, Father, forgive them; for they know not what they do."[1] Now, as He stands before the Father as our advocate,[2] He may well be saying the same thing with a bit of a twist: "Father, forgive them; for they do not what they know."

There is something in human nature that allows us to go on doing, time and again, things we know are not right, or at least not the best for us to do. This is particularly true if our less-than-best behavior is not illegal or harmful to others and we are not forced to change. I am not sure I could come up with detailed instructions for an easily followed, step-by-step approach to becoming who we ought to be, but perhaps a few thoughts will be helpful as you prepare for your mission and the rest of your life.

First of all, it is important to realize that the goal is to be who we are, not who we think somebody else is or who others may want us to be. The obligation we have to ourselves is to develop what is in us, who we are inside. Others may give us input in the process, but no one else can really know what and how we should be. They can know their own reaction to our behavior or make their own assessment of the correctness of what we do, but they can only surmise how well it fits with our own thoughts and feelings about who we are. We are all unique and should glory in that uniqueness.

In knowing that, though, it is also important to realize that there is nothing wrong with some dependence and some con-formity—some fitting in. It is perfectly normal for us to lean on one another for assistance. None of us is in this life alone. We all need the love and support of others. It should also be

---

1. Luke 23:34.
2. See Doctrine and Covenants 45:3–5.

acceptable to us to set aside some of our self-centered ideas and align ourselves with principles of behavior that lead to the well-being of the whole group. Missionaries have plenty of rules, lots of things they are expected to do, from white shirts and conservative ties to bedtime at 10:30 to no swimming. This kind of conforming is called obedience and will serve you very well.

In becoming who we are, we should be careful not to lose our dignity in the name of individuality. We should not forget that propriety is important. Even when we know our heart is right, there is a lot to be said for acting and looking that way, too. The more we fit in with the society of which we choose to be a part, the more likely we are to be successful in the culture of that group. Little signs of behavior that might be considered rebellious, even though seemingly harmless, may allow people to take us less seriously than we hope they would. If you act like a servant of the Lord, you will be seen that way by others.

Remember that self-development is an ongoing process, not a single event. It happens a little at a time, as we learn how to do it. In fact, it really lasts a lifetime. People who expect to be everything all at once are generally quite frustrated. On the other hand, those who don't expect enough of themselves fail to make much progress. They often end up wishing they had done more, tried harder, and pushed themselves further. They are frequently jealous of the accomplishments of those who did pay the price for success. The key is achieving a good balance—doing our best, but not expecting more of ourselves than is reasonable.

Another very important factor is limits. One of the most exciting things about becoming an adult is freedom from many of the limits that were imposed by parents and other caregivers.

The natural tendency, as soon as we get some freedom, is to resist the imposition of limitations on what we can do. That is all right to a degree, but not when it leads to excess or irresponsibility.

The most successful people set their own limits. They don't necessarily do what they do because someone told them to, but because they want to do it that way. They set their own reasonable limits and choose to live within them. Compared to what they did at home, they may be stricter with themselves in some areas and less strict in others, but the limits are theirs. They are in reality doing what they want to do. It may not be what they *could* do, what they are capable of doing given no limits, but they have chosen, in their pursuit of success, to limit themselves in certain areas. The interesting thing is that these kinds of limits will result in greater freedom down the road. A person who limits spending and instead saves a little will have more money later in life and far greater financial freedom than the one who has no early limits.

I hesitate to use the word that best describes this limit setting because of the bad vibrations it causes in many people, but the word is *discipline.* Discipline is the foundation of success. Disciplined eaters and exercisers are generally more physically fit. Disciplined spenders are wealthier. Disciplined followers of the Lord are disciples indeed, and worthily loving and serving others. Those without some discipline usually wish they could be like those who have it. Again, however, balance is important. We determine the level of success we desire and then practice the level of discipline that will allow us to achieve it. And the level will vary as circumstances change in our lives. It is sad to see missionaries who keep saying they will practice discipline, but who keep putting it off in a very undisciplined manner and then wind up frustrated and disappointed with their mission experience.

Much of our sadness in life is based on wishing things were different. Undisciplined people are almost always wishing things were different. Those who have some balanced discipline in their lives may still want things to be a bit different, but, because of the limits within which they live, they see progress and maintain a lively hope that they will eventually have what they want. Deep down, undisciplined people feel a lot of hopelessness. In the back of their minds, they know they will not have what they want because they are not doing what it takes to have it.

The last thing I would suggest is to have some focus. Even if it is quite broad and general, some direction is very important. Discipline provides momentum, but without direction we leave our destination to luck or to chance, and the odds are heavily against our arriving where we would want to be. Direction does not have to be unwavering. We can change direction anytime we need to. In fact, minor adjustments may be important as we gain a more clear understanding of where we want to end up.

In summary, the successful transition into adulthood would seem to be achieved through:

- appreciating and trusting our uniqueness
- accepting some dependence and conformity
- being patient with ourselves
- creating limits and disciplining ourselves
- developing a general sense of direction

Missionary life is full of challenges, rough roads, accidents, mistakes, and surprises, but the good times far outweigh the hard times. All of life can be a wonderful adventure in learning, sharing, dreaming, failing, starting over, and achieving. My young friend is in for a real treat as a full-time missionary, and it will be all the more sweet for her as she incorporates the principles mentioned here. I think she will do it. After all, she was smart enough to ask how.

In Their Own Words

The members of our little branch were stellar, but the missionary work was not going so well. The members wanted to help, so they started a "forty-day fast." Over a forty-day period, each member of the branch was assigned to fast on one particular day. We all put our trust in the Lord. When the fast started, we had only three progressing investigators, there were no baptismal dates scheduled, and we were teaching about four lessons per week. However, because of the faith of the branch members and the fast they were doing, we saw how much it could change. By the end of the fast, we had ten progressing investigators and eight baptismal dates scheduled, and we were teaching fifteen to twenty lessons per week. The faith of the members launched missionary work! That was one of the big miracles of my mission, and it helped me know that God is in charge and that Jesus Christ is the head of this Church. He leads the missionary efforts depending on our faith and His timing. I know this to be true.

Chapter 21

COMMON COURTESY

E arly in his life, George Washington wrote down a list of what he described as the rules of civility. The first of these guidelines for good manners suggested that "every action done in company [of other people] ought to be with some sign of respect, to those that are present."[1] Young George learned the importance of acting with courtesy toward others. This lesson is essential for missionaries.

Courtesy is kindness come alive. Courtesy is shown by the driver who slows so that other cars can merge. It lives in the person who stands on a crowded bus to give a seat to one who needs it more. Courtesy is displayed whenever we do even a small kindness that shows respect, or makes life a little easier, or brightens the day of someone else. Of a man known for his

---

1. George Washington, *Rules of Civility & Decent Behaviour in Company and Conversation: A Book of Etiquette* (1971), 22.

courtesy it was said, "Yesterday was dark and rainy, but [he] passed [by] and the sun shone."[2]

As a missionary, your actions will be judged almost constantly. Not that you, yourself, will be judged, but the Church and your message will be judged by your behavior. Two missionaries who were going door to door met a woman who invited them in. As they entered, she explained that some months before that time she had watched two missionaries who did not even know she noticed them. Their behavior was so kind and they had such good manners that she said to herself, "I hope my sons will grow up to be men like that." She invited the missionaries into her home to learn what it was that made them so courteous.

Perhaps the most enduring law of relationships has been called "The Golden Rule." Simply stated, it suggests that we treat others as we would hope to be treated.[3] When we are courteous and act with thoughtful kindness, those around us are likely to respond toward us in the same way.

Common courtesy may not be as common as it used to be, but each of us can do our part to keep it alive by letting the spirit of civility guide our every action—even when we don't think anyone is watching.

In Their Own Words

While serving in St. Denis, a suburb of Paris, my companion and I experienced a small miracle that helped us know that Father in Heaven is always aware of each one of us.

---

2. Sister Mary Mercedes, *A Book of Courtesy: The Art of Living With Yourself and Others* (1910), 1.
3. See Matthew 7:12.

It was a fast Sunday and one of our first meetings of the day was a missionary coordination meeting. In that meeting, the Relief Society president mentioned that a young adult woman had moved into our ward boundaries and that the ward needed to get into contact with her. The ward appeared to take charge of the fellowship, and my companion and I continued in the meeting without further thought.

After church that morning, we had scheduled an appointment with an investigator. The appointment was not far from our apartment, and we arrived only to find out that our investigator was not there. We headed back to our apartment, and on our way back we received a call from our next appointment asking us to come early.

We jumped onto the next available bus and headed to the train station. Customarily, at this train station we would stand in the middle of the platform and wait for the next train. However, on this day, for no particular reason, as it seemed to us, we veered to the far side of the platform and took a seat. Not long after sitting down we heard a woman's voice ask, "Elders?"

To our surprise we realized that it was the young adult woman who had been mentioned in our earlier missionary coordination meeting. We were able to get her contact information to pass on to the ward and to have a small discussion as we waited for the next train.

The story may seem minor in significance, but to us it was miraculous. Here was a young woman new to the area, in a place where the Church can be hard to find, where fellowship from fellow members is critical. It worked out so that we would be at the train station at the same time as this woman. Meeting at the train station at the same time is even more miraculous when one considers that trains are passing by every ten to twelve minutes and there are hundreds of passengers entering and exiting the trains per hour.

For my companion and me, it was a demonstration that on the Lord's errand we can be guided to those who need us most, and He will orchestrate the circumstances perfectly.

Chapter 22

SURVIVING THE "WILDERNESS"

When Moses first left Egypt, he traveled into the wilderness.[1] We don't know a great deal about his life there, but we can suppose that whatever experiences he had were designed by the Lord to prepare him for his role as Israel's prophet. The wilderness years were a vital part of his development. We all need a little time in the "wilderness" to toughen us, humble us, and teach us the lessons that will serve us well in the future.

Years ago, I knew a young man named David who was incredibly frustrated by the computer illiteracy that seemed like a black plague that had settled over the small town where he lived and killed off any chance for his happiness. "What am I going to do?" he questioned. "No one here gets it. There's no one to help me and no one to even talk to about programming! If only we lived in a bigger place." These were pre-Internet

---

1. See Exodus 2.

days. How exasperated and lonely he felt, isolated in a technology no-man's-land with seemingly no resources for rescue.

Then one day he went in to browse at the local store that sold computer hardware. The store had plenty of inventory, but the owners were really just businessmen, not computer geeks to whom David could relate. But then the unforeseen occurred.

"Can I help you, young man?" asked the owner.

"No, thanks, just looking," David replied.

"Do you know much about computers?" inquired the man.

"Well, yes," was David's bold reply, "but there really isn't much to do with them here. What we need is networking."

"Networking!" said the man. "I've been reading about that. A network would help us sell computers. What would we need to do to start one?"

Well, he didn't have to ask twice. David and he spent quite some time discussing the process of establishing a computer network in their little town. By the end of the conversation, David had a job, and the computer network he dreamed of was launched. He was soon bicycling all over town helping several businesses and the Board of Education set up their networks. This is something that very likely never would have happened in a big-city environment with plenty of resources and computer-savvy kids. David needed the experience to be gained in the "wilderness." The knowledge he received there served as a foundation for academic and professional achievement that has taken him to the heights of computer science. He now works as a highly paid software architect in the southeastern United States, a far cry from the computer desert in which he felt so lost.

Sometimes it is from what seems like the wasteland of life that we gain the greatest learning. Prophets and hermits have gone to the wilderness to find meaning and inspiration. I love it when, in the movie, Ben Hur is released from the desperation of the slave galley having learned what he needed to fulfill his destiny. It is inspiring to see an athlete or a politician or a business person come from a life of deprivation to become a great success. The theme of learning the most when all seems to be lost is played out over and over again in fiction and, much more meaningfully, in real life.

When life seems hopeless, stop and look around. Figure out what you might learn from where you are. What does this miserable or tragic experience have to teach you? What good can you gain from this difficult time? It may not be obvious. It may take more time and further experience for you to finally see it clearly, but it is there—that element which was missing from your character, which has now been placed there by the sometimes heavy, occasionally painful hand of life. Sparkling diamonds are created in oppressive heat with excessive pressure.

As a missionary, you may be assigned to a challenging companion or a city where the work is especially difficult. Count your blessings! Cheerfully go about your work and trust in the inspiration of your mission president. Learn what you can and thank the Lord that He thought enough of you to give you a "wilderness" experience.

In Their Own Words

I have seen countless miracles during my time as a missionary. They range from individual appointments to baptisms. For me, the greatest miracle is my own conversion. That sounds conceited, but it's true. I thought I had a solid foundation and testimony before my mission, but compared to now, it was sturdy, but not solid. I feel like I learned more from the people I helped teach than they did from me. The principles of the gospel are now woven into my soul. My faith has increased and the plan of salvation has become a reality, not just something I learned in Sunday School. Watching how the gospel has changed the lives of others, right before my eyes, has also changed mine.

Chapter 23

A MERRY HEART

A woman and her daughter cheerfully left the hospital room of their very ill mother and grandmother. "How come," said the young girl, "when we go visit Grandma to make her happy, she cheers *us* up? She's the one who's sick, but she makes *us* feel better."

"She has always been that way," replied her mother. "Her body isn't well, but she still has a happy heart."

Even in her illness, this good woman was able to maintain a cheerful disposition. She had learned the important lesson that despite the setbacks and difficult experiences of life, we can maintain a feeling of peace and joy. She believed the ancient proverb that states, "A merry heart doeth good like a medicine."[1]

At times when it would be so easy and perhaps understandable for us to give in to pessimism and a bleak outlook on life, we can realize that though our physical comfort might be taken from us and our worldly possessions may be lost, no one can rob us of our good cheer. Generally, personal happiness is

1. Proverbs 17:22.

not stolen; it is given away, surrendered to circumstances that seem to demand that we yield our contentment and stop being happy. How valuable the knowledge that even in the midst of significant suffering, we can keep our good spirits!

One of the most remarkable points about going on a mission is the fact that you will, almost all at once, give up many of the things that seemed so important to you. These will include movies, TV, most of your music, hobbies, dating, even time with your closest friends and family. It can be tough to set these things aside. When you do, you will begin to understand what the stake president meant when he said he was "setting you apart" as a full-time missionary. You will truly be set apart from many of the things of the world. Your call letter will say, "You will also be expected to devote all your time and attention to serving the Lord, leaving behind all other personal affairs."[2] That represents a big change! Having a "merry heart" will help you see the bright side of what may feel like a sacrifice.

Also in your call letter, the President of the Church promises, "As you do these things the Lord will bless you and you will become an effective advocate and messenger of the truth."[3] Your full-time missionary service can be the happiest time of your life.

I recall a fine elder who was having a difficult time keeping all the mission rules. He did pretty well with everything but music. "President," he said, "I'll die without my music!" He wanted to be obedient, but he didn't think he could. He was frustrated with himself and not as dedicated to the work as he should have been. I was inspired to assign him to an apartment

---

2. *Preach My Gospel: A Guide to Missionary Service* (2004), 137.
3. *Preach My Gospel,* 137.

with two sets of missionaries. The other team was the zone leaders, and I knew they wouldn't allow any unauthorized music to be played in that apartment. The troubled elder had to give up his music cold turkey—and he didn't die! Soon he felt better about himself. His heart was merry, he became more focused, and he was a much better missionary. It wasn't long before he was called to a leadership position, where he served as an example to other missionaries.

When the sun sets on the easy times, the light in our heart can still radiate gladness. When we feel like things are hard, the tonic of a "merry heart" may be just the right cure for the ailments of life.

In Their Own Words

Learning a new language can be daunting. I remember my stake president in my home setting me apart to serve in the France Paris Mission. France?! . . . I had taken every other language in school but French! How could I learn a language in which I had no background? Yet, as done so often for other missionaries, my stake president blessed me with the gift of tongues. I remember pondering how this gift would be realized on my mission. I had dreams of one day waking up and speaking the language perfectly and as easily as my native language. Or, would it happen so gradually that I wouldn't even recognize it? Serving in my first area in France, I soon learned that language creates barriers, but the language of the Spirit can overcome all obstacles.

However, as a "Bleue" or new sister missionary in France, and desiring with all my heart to share the gospel that meant so much to me, I was frustrated with my slow ability to learn the language. We were teaching a family a member had introduced to us. She was a single mom with two boys around the ages of six and eight. I could see in their eyes the love they were developing for the gospel. It brought a light in their lives, and they were eager to learn more. As we taught them, my heart was full of love and a longing for them to be able to more fully partake of the blessings the gospel has to offer.

In one of our first lessons, we taught the plan of salvation. As we started the lesson, and then as my companion took over teaching, I looked into our investigator's eyes. The Spirit told me she wasn't understanding. I could see she was becoming distant. There was a feeling of confusion, and it almost felt like the room was full of chaos. In that moment, I prayed more fervently and asked Heavenly Father that we would have the Spirit with us and she would be able to understand. I told Heavenly Father how much I loved this family and wanted them to understand. I started talking and, although I was new and just learning French, it was like my mind was opened up and the words just flowed. I was able to clearly and simply explain the plan of salvation. There came a point as I spoke that I started to stumble over my French once more, and I knew that I was once again left to myself. It was like the part of my mind that had opened up had a curtain drawn over it again. As I looked at my investigator, the Spirit told me that she understood, and there was a calm that came into the room.

Thanks to this experience, I know Heavenly Father cares for all His children and wants them to have the blessings of peace and calm in their lives. I also know Heavenly Father was showing me that although I was struggling with all sincerity to learn French, He was with me and He fulfills His promises. Doctrine and Covenants 84:88 puts it beautifully, "And whoso receiveth you, there I will be also, for I will go before your face. I will be on your right hand and on your left, and my spirit shall be in your hearts, and mine angels round about you, to bear you up." How grateful I am for a gospel that promises us that God will be with us.

Chapter 24

THE VIRTUE OF HUMILITY

In his autobiography, Benjamin Franklin tells of his strong desire to develop a worthy character. To do this, he made a list of the twelve virtues he most wanted to achieve and then came up with a plan to practice each one on a regular basis. After learning of the plan, a friend suggested that Ben Franklin add one more virtue to his list, one that many felt he needed. He agreed, and added it—humility. Later on in life, he wrote that it was the practice of humility that allowed him to have such great influence for good.[1]

Humility means setting aside our personal interests in favor of giving careful attention to what others need or what they may have to offer. Humility is not exclusive to any particular class or type of people. Anyone can be humble. We can start by carefully listening to what others have to say. A humble person knows that we all have a lot to learn and that we can learn something meaningful from almost anyone. A person with humility doesn't care who gets the credit, as long as the right thing is done.

---

1. See *The Autobiography of Benjamin Franklin* (1888), 101–14.

As Ben Franklin tried to be humble, he found that he was less inclined to judge others before hearing them out. He was less likely to argue that his opinion was the only one that could be right. He was gentler in his efforts to persuade others and more open to new ideas.

As St. Augustine, an early Catholic priest, said, "Do you wish to rise? Begin by descending. You plan a tower that will pierce the clouds? Lay first the foundation of humility."[2]

I once heard President Boyd K. Packer say, "In the kingdom of God, the way up is down." Think about it!

It's hard to know if you're humble. Just when you think you are, you probably aren't. But if you look upon others as equals, if you try to think of others before yourself, if the thoughts, opinions, and feelings of other people really matter to you, you are likely well on your way to developing the precious virtue of humility.

In Their Own Words

On my first Sunday in the mission field, my companion and trainer was telling me how we would have to meet the bishopric and the members and make a good impression. I was a bit nervous about it all, but he told me I would be fine. He shared with me his first Sunday in the mission field. "I went to church and met someone there who I baptized not long after. You will find someone today who will be baptized." I figured his hope knew no bounds!

I thought to myself that the only people I would

---

2. Accessed online at http://www.brainyquote.com/quotes/keywords/humility.

meet who would be baptized were probably going to be some 7¾-year-old kids in the ward. So, expecting a nonmiraculous day, but still praying my companion would be right, I went to the ward meetings for the first time.

Priesthood and Sunday School went by quickly. During the switch from Sunday School to sacrament meeting, I saw several sevenish-looking kids, but no investigator. At the end of sacrament meeting, we were about to leave when we saw the elders quorum president talking to someone. We decided to introduce ourselves. We walked over, and the president said, "Ah! Just the people we need." He pointed to the man he was speaking to and said, "Elders, meet Steven." The man said, "Hello. My name is Steven and I am interested in joining your church." Two months later, I baptized Steven.

Chapter 25

PURE SERVICE

Remember that the purpose of missionary work is to "invite others to come unto Christ by helping them."[1] It often seems that those who really are helpful and who do the most good for others do so quietly. They don't wear their goodness like a medal and call attention to their acts of charity or even bravery. They proclaim their goodness by what they do and let their example speak for itself.

Mother Teresa, a Catholic sister who spent her life serving the poorest of the poor and doing good to all she met, took very little credit for her remarkable service. When praised for her work she said, "I am just a little pencil in [God's] hand."[2] She pointed out that "there should be less talk" and more action. "Take a broom and clean someone's house," she taught. "That says enough."[3]

Those who leave a legacy of good deeds generally shun the limelight. They would rather modestly push a broom, or

---

1. *Preach My Gospel: A Guide to Missionary Service* (2004), 1.

2. Mother Teresa, *No Greater Love* (1997), 53.

3. Accessed online at http://mothertheresasayings.com/sayings.htm.

quietly bind up a wound, or lend a private shoulder to cry on than bask in the praise of those who would send adulation their way. President Gordon B. Hinckley used to say, "Adulation is poison." By that he meant that praise can go to your head and cause you to lose your humility.

Make it a practice to try to serve anonymously. As much as possible, don't let anyone know of the good things you do. The kindest actions and the best people are often noticed only by the ones they serve. You can trust, however, that Heavenly Father sees and really appreciates all the good you do.

"Verily I say unto you, Inasmuch as ye have done it unto one of the least of these my brethren, ye have done it unto me."[4]

"And behold, I tell you these things that ye may learn wisdom; that ye may learn that when ye are in the service of your fellow beings ye are only in the service of your God."[5]

In Their Own Words

As we were teaching a man who had emigrated from Africa, we invited him to come to church. He told us that he didn't have enough money for the bus fare. We invited him to pray and to be confident that the Lord would provide a way for him. That Sunday he was at church and he explained the miracle.

He lived out of town and far from the chapel. He really wanted to come to church, but still he was without money. He trusted the Lord and made the very long walk to catch the bus. When the bus came, he stepped on and told the driver he was without any money. The

---

4. Matthew 25:40.
5. Mosiah 2:17.

driver talked to him and asked why he needed to go into town. Our investigator explained that he needed to go to church. The driver shared that he was a believer as well, and he gave to our friend ten travel tickets without charge. The Lord provides the miracle after we exercise our faith.

Chapter 26

CHOOSE NOT TO BE OFFENDED

Much of the joy we experience in life comes from our interaction with other people. Almost all of your associations with other missionaries will be pleasant and cause little or no distress, but every now and then something may happen that results in your being offended and hurt by the actions of others. This can be especially true for young men and women who are not used to being 24/7 with a companion.

Offense comes when the behavior of another person runs counter to what we hoped would happen, and we become annoyed. When these painful things occur, we have a choice to make. We can choose to harbor feelings of resentment, or we can choose to deal with the offense in a constructive way and let go of the negative feelings.

It is normal to have feelings of offense, but hanging on to those feelings and letting them grow is not required. In fact, though we may be the victim of someone else's thoughtlessness, we can be victimized a second time by our own choice to hold on to our hurt feelings. Even if we can't escape being offended, we can at least avoid the results.

It is far better to make the choice to recognize the suffering caused by bad feelings and then, with kindness and compassion for yourself and for the offending party, find a way to resolve the matter positively. As we read in Proverbs, "A soft answer turneth away wrath,"[1] and as the Psalmist said, "Great peace have they which love thy law: and nothing shall offend them."[2] The initial pain of offense may be inevitable, but the ongoing suffering is optional, if we simply choose not to be offended.

In Their Own Words

In our spiritual planning session, we prayed to know where the Lord would have us work the next day. We both felt strongly that we should visit the local university campus. This seemed to be a strange thing, because that day was a holiday and the university would be closed, but we decided to go anyway.

When we arrived on the campus, it was almost deserted. All the buildings were closed. We walked around the grounds for about forty-five minutes without seeing anyone we could contact. We began to wonder why we were there and considered moving on. All of a sudden we saw a man coming toward us. I said to my companion, "Maybe this is the man we are supposed to meet. Let's speak to him."

As we approached the man, his face lit up as if he recognized us. We greeted him, and he said, "My name is

---

1. Proverbs 15:1.
2. Psalm 119:165.

Randy. I was taught by the missionaries in another town, but when I moved here I lost track of them." We quickly made an appointment to meet with Randy.

Several weeks later, Randy was baptized. The Lord knew where he would be and directed us to be in his path at the right time. From this experience we learned to trust the impressions of the Spirit and to trust our own ability to listen!

Chapter 27

WHEN YOU OFFEND SOMEONE

It is extremely important that missionary companions get along. President Gordon B. Hinckley told the story of his first missionary companion. The senior elder said to young Elder Hinckley, "We'll get along great as long as you remember that everything I have is mine and everything you have is mine!" Of course, he was kidding, but sometime during your mission you might act as if that were true and do something—drink his milk, eat her cookie, offer "constructive" criticism, use her shampoo without asking, or whatever—to offend your companion.

Ella Wheeler Wilcox probably wrote from personal experience when she said:

> *One great truth in life I've found,*
> *While journeying to the West—*
> *The only folks we really wound*
> *Are those we love the best.*[1]

---

1. "Those We Love the Best," in *Poems That Touch the Heart,* comp. A. L. Alexander (1956), 166.

It is true that by a careless word or a thoughtless or self-ish act we may do harm even to those who are precious to us. A troubled companionship will have a hard time receiving the blessings of the Spirit they really need. And if we don't do something to correct the problem, the work and our joy in it can be seriously damaged.

The key to repairing much of the hurt can be summed up in two words: "I'm sorry." It takes a wise and strong person to say these words, and it may be hard to do, but a renewal of love and friendship is worth it. Life is too short and friendships are too few to waste time fighting or holding a grudge when an apology will set things right.

W. W. Phelps was a prominent member of the Church in the early days. He wrote the words to many of our favorite hymns, including "The Spirit of God," which was originally sung at the dedication of the Kirtland Temple. At one point he was offended by what he thought to be wrong behavior by some of the leaders of the Church. He reacted to his hurt feel-ings by spreading lies about his former companions and even putting their lives in danger. Later, when he was finally able to recognize his errors, see how much he had lost, and realize how he wanted to rebuild those friendships, he wrote to Joseph Smith, saying, "I have done wrong and I am sorry." Quick to forgive, the Prophet Joseph wrote to Brother Phelps and said, "Come on, dear brother . . . for friends at first, are friends again at last."[2]

Perhaps nothing we say can do more good in a bad situation than "I'm sorry." These few words can overcome anger and

---

2. Joseph Smith, *History of the Church of Jesus Christ of Latter-day Saints,* 7 vols. (1974), 4:142, 164.

help mend a broken heart. An apology, when followed by sincere effort to avoid the problem in the future, can bring peace and put derailed relationships back on track. Even if we think we aren't at fault, if we apologize for whatever we might have done to contribute to the hurt, "friends at first" can be "friends again at last."

So, when necessary, apologize, say you're truly sorry, and let the healing begin.

In Their Own Words

I arrived in the mission field in March, so all of my shirts were long-sleeved. I figured I could get some short-sleeved shirts when it started to get warmer. One day, I had the idea that I could just have the sleeves of my shirts cut off. Then I wouldn't have to buy new ones. "But, Elder," said my companion, "then you'll just have to buy more long-sleeved shirts when it gets cold again. Just buy some new short-sleeved shirts and you'll be fine." He was right, of course, but I just couldn't get out of my mind the need to have my shirts altered.

One day we were walking down the street and passed by a dry cleaner's shop. In the window was a sign saying that they also did alterations. We went a little farther down the street and I said to my companion, "Let's go back. I just want to see what it would cost to have my shirts altered." For some reason it seemed really important to me. My companion must have thought I was crazy, but he was nice enough to turn around and go back with me to the dry cleaner's.

When we entered the shop, before we could say anything, the woman behind the counter said, "Do you smoke?" We answered, "No." She then said, "Do you drink?" Again, we said, "No." "Good," she said. "I have been trying to quit smoking and drinking, but haven't been able to. When I saw you walk by in front of the store, I said a quick prayer that, if you were the ones who could help me, you would come back. And you did."

We started teaching this woman and she was able to quit drinking and smoking. She was later baptized.

Chapter 28

FIND JOY IN WORK

At the funeral service of his father, a middle-aged man stood to express his feelings. "Father provided well for our family," he said. "He always made sure we had what we needed, but the greatest gift he gave me was teaching me how to work." With tears in his eyes he continued, "Dad loved us, and he showed that love by helping us learn the joy of a hard day's work and a job well done."

One mission president said, "I love to get new missionaries who are Idaho farm boys. They know how to work!" Of course, not all hard workers were raised on a farm, but you get the picture. Missionary work can be tough, and those who have learned to work hard and find joy in it have gained something that will be helpful.

I had odd jobs before my first mission, including construction work, which was difficult in the summer heat, but I really learned how to work hard as a full-time missionary. Construction work paid well. We did missionary work for free. In fact, we paid for the privilege! But in missionary work, perhaps the hardest I have ever done, the reward was truly great. It came in the form of satisfaction in doing our best, joy in seeing others change for the better, and knowing that the Lord was pleased with us.

The work was made easier and more joyful because we were dedicated to the cause of righteousness and establishing the kingdom of God. When times were hard for the early Church, the Prophet Joseph encouraged everyone to keep going and to be happy. He wrote, "Brethren [and sisters], shall we not go on in so great a cause? Go forward and not backward. Courage, brethren; and on, on to the victory! Let your hearts rejoice, and be exceedingly glad. Let the earth break forth into singing."[1]

So, dear brothers and sisters, let's get to work. Prepare well for your mission. Serve honorably with faith, obedience, and diligence. Love every minute of it. You'll be blessed if you do this, now and for the rest of your life, even your eternal life. God bless that it may be so.

In Their Own Words

To me a miracle is something that is so perfect, only God's love and grace could be the answer to why things happened the way they did. Missionaries are blessed to witness miracles each and every day. Every miracle I witnessed on my mission, like this one, will always be so special to me.

In an effort to become more efficient missionaries, my companion and I made the goal to be more in tune with the Spirit. We had a testimony that people were being prepared for the gospel, and we wanted to show

---

1. Doctrine and Covenants 128:22.

our faith by asking for promptings of how to find those prepared people. Each morning after our studies we would sincerely pray for promptings and then share our feelings with each other. One day we felt like we should keep our eyes open for a lamp. An hour later we visited with a woman carrying a lamp on the metro. Each day we had learned to follow these promptings and were receiving the fruits of our faith and work. On one particular day my companion told me that she envisioned stilts and popcorn, like at a carnival. I told her that I had a feeling children's books might be important. They were strange promptings, but we were confident that they came from the Spirit.

On our way to our first appointment that morning we felt prompted to take the tram [surface train] instead of the metro [subway]. On the tram ride we noticed that a big carnival had just moved to the town square that day. Right after our appointment we went to the carnival and talked to everyone we saw. After about an hour of talking with uninterested people we found a tall teenage boy who was very interested in our message. We talked for almost an hour about many aspects of the gospel and answered several questions that he had. In getting to know him we learned that he and his friends were involved in carnival events, specifically an act on stilts. We also noticed that where we found him was right next to the popcorn machine, across the street from a children's book store. We continued to teach this boy over the next few months. This experience made it so clear to me that Heavenly Father knows and loves each one of His children. He prepares them for the gospel so that when they're ready they will find it. If we ask for it, the Spirit will literally guide us where we need to go.

Chapter 29

ONWARD AND UPWARD

In the April 2000 general conference of the Church, President Boyd K. Packer related the following parable:

"A merchant man seeking precious jewels found at last the perfect pearl. He had the finest craftsman carve a superb jewel box and line it with blue velvet. He put his pearl of great price on display so others could share his treasure. He watched as people came to see it. Soon he turned away in sorrow. It was the box they admired, not the pearl."[1]

Imagine the value of "the perfect pearl." It would be worth a real fortune! The worth of the box, as beautiful and important as it certainly was, would be far less than that of the pearl. So why did the people who viewed the pearl in the box pay more attention to the thing of lesser value? First let's discover the meaning of the objects in the parable.

The pearl seems to represent the thing of greatest worth, like the pure gospel of Jesus Christ. The box might represent the good things of this world that can serve as a distraction from that which is of most value. President Packer put it this

---

1. "The Cloven Tongues of Fire," *Ensign*, May 2000, 7.

way, "I fear this supernal gift [the pearl] is being obscured by programs and activities and schedules and so many meetings [the box]. There are so many places to go, so many things to do in this noisy world. We can be too busy to pay attention to the promptings of the Spirit."[2] We tend to get so caught up in the demands of everyday life that we lose track of the things that matter most.

In missionary work, you will have the opportunity to present to people the "pearl of great price."[3] The gem you will offer them is the gospel of Jesus Christ. When they are converted and want to be baptized, it should be because they have gained a testimony of the gospel, not because we have nice meetinghouses with pretty pictures on the wall (as nice as those are), or because we have a great welfare program (as important as that is), or because you and your companion are so good and kind (though you may well be). Some people are attracted by the social experience in the Church. Others come because they think it will please someone they care about. True conversion, however, is a personal, heartfelt, spiritual experience that comes from the Holy Ghost and is not based simply on outward, earthly things. Your task will be to assist your investigators to see beyond "the box" and to learn to understand and love "the pearl." You must teach the gospel, also called the doctrine, of Christ. In order to teach it, you should understand what the gospel is and how it fits into our lives.

The gospel of Jesus Christ as declared by Him and His disciples consists of five elements:

---

2. "Cloven Tongues of Fire," 8.
3. Matthew 13:46.

1. Faith in Jesus Christ
2. Repentance
3. Baptism (receiving ordinances and making covenants)
4. Receiving the Holy Ghost
5. Enduring to the end (remaining obedient to covenants)

All other doctrines and practices are supportive of or derived from these five principles of the gospel. Everything we have or do in the Church is based on the application of these foundational tenets in the lives of individual people. These principles represent "the fulness of the gospel of Jesus Christ."[4] They are "the pearl of great price."

The table below will give you some references from two chapters in the Book of Mormon in which the gospel is defined by the Lord Himself, even with some emphasis by the Father. These chapters and others are definitely worth studying.

The Gospel of Jesus Christ	
Faith in Jesus Christ	
2 Nephi 31:13	Follow the Son, with full purpose of heart.
2 Nephi 31:20–21	Press forward in Christ. There is no other name given whereby man can be saved.
3 Nephi 27:14	Jesus was sent to accomplish the Atonement.
Repentance	
2 Nephi 31:13	Repent of your sins.
3 Nephi 27:20	Repent, all ye ends of the earth.
Baptism	
2 Nephi 31:13	Witness that you are willing to take upon yourself the name of Christ by baptism.
3 Nephi 27:20	Come unto Christ and be baptized.

---

4. Doctrine and Covenants 20:9.

The Gospel of Jesus Christ	
The Gift of the Holy Ghost	
2 Nephi 31:13	Then you shall receive the Holy Ghost.
3 Nephi 27:20	That ye may be sanctified by the reception of the Holy Ghost.
Endure to the end	
2 Nephi 31:20	Press forward and endure to the end.
3 Nephi 27:16	Endure to the end.

It seems to be a common misconception that receiving the gospel is kind of a step-by-step, linear process. First you have faith, then you repent and get baptized, then comes the companionship of the Holy Ghost, then you just endure. In a sense that is true, but there is more to it than that. Rather than being a straight-line progression from Point A (faith) to Point E (enduring), perhaps the process is more like an upward spiral.

Think of it this way: Baptism is the first of the saving ordinances. There are others. For instance, receiving the temple endowment and being sealed to a spouse are also required for exaltation. So, instead of limiting the gospel ordinances to baptism, let's include all the ordinances of salvation and exaltation. In addition, it seems easier to understand what endurance means if we just refer to that element of the gospel as ongoing obedience.

As we develop faith in the Lord, repent, get baptized, receive the Holy Ghost, and remain obedient, what happens to us? Our faith in Jesus increases. That makes us want to repent even more. We then are worthy to receive higher ordinances, like the endowment, which increases the influence of the Holy Ghost in our lives and helps us be more obedient. Then our faith in Jesus deepens and we seek even more careful repentance. This brings more of the Spirit into our lives and we become more and more obedient. On and on we go, applying the same principles of the gospel, but in a more refined and intelligent way. We don't just stay at the same level. As we progress and apply the doctrine of Christ in our lives, we rise higher and higher and closer and closer to the Lord, until someday we can become like Him. Living the gospel is not a straight and flat process, but an exciting and challenging upward spiral, carrying us up and up to finally dwell in the presence of our Heavenly Father and His Beloved Son.

Of course, you will be teaching much more than just the five elements of the gospel. You will teach about Joseph Smith, the Book of Mormon, the Apostasy, the Word of Wisdom, and many other points of doctrine. These are important parts of the whole package we refer to as the restored gospel. Just don't lose sight of the fact that the simple gospel of Jesus Christ contains all the essentials and is the foundation upon which true testimonies are built. It is where real conversion occurs.

Now just a word about the progressive nature of ordinances and covenants. With each covenant we make, we offer more of ourselves to the Lord. As we progress in receiving ordinances and making covenants, our level of commitment will increase and, along with that, our responsibility to the keep the covenants we have made will also grow. Remember, "of him unto whom much is given much is required."[5] It helps me to see it as follows:

---

5. Doctrine and Covenants 82:3.

The Ordinance	The Covenant	My Offering
Baptism	Compassion	Personal service to others[6]
Endowment	Consecration	Everything I have to the Church[7] (part of this is receiving the Melchizedek Priesthood with an oath and covenant)[8]
Sealing	Continuation	I give my very self to my spouse[9] (this allows for exaltation and the continuation of the family)[10]

Compassion, the desire to help others, may at this point in your life be your primary motivation for serving a mission. Once you have received your endowment—a wonderful gift of knowledge and covenant making—a feeling of consecration will come into your heart, and your desire to serve the Lord and your fellow men will grow. Sometime in the future, you will have the privilege of entering the temple and making eternal promises to the Father and to a worthy son or daughter of God. As you keep your promises, Heavenly Father will fulfill His, and you will have a continuation of family life forever. You will contribute to the glory of the Father, and your joy will increase for all eternity.

6. See Mosiah 18:8–10.
7. See Doctrine and Covenants 42:30; 104:11–18.
8. See Doctrine and Covenants 84:33–40.
9. See Doctrine and Covenants 42:22.
10. See Doctrine and Covenants 132:30–31.

In Their Own Words

In our mission we were taught to do consecrated finding, meaning we prayed to visualize a specific person we were to find during the day so that we had a little extra direction and motivation to find the characteristic that came to mind before we went out (sometimes it was a skin or hair color, a purse color, shoe color, and so on). One day my companion and I had other plans fall through, so before we left our apartment after lunch we prayed about who to find and where to go looking. We said multiple prayers and were pondering over the map of our area and closing our eyes to imagine what person we should look for, and nothing was coming to either of us. We kept trying, talking through possibilities and trying to rule any options in or out, but we weren't sure where to go or who to look for. I can't remember how long we tried but we finally decided that we needed to simply get out of the apartment; we weren't accomplishing anything in the apartment, so we needed to move and we would be led as we went. I'm not sure if we were expecting an answer to immediately come to mind the moment we stepped out the door, but if that's what we were expecting that wasn't what we got. We kind of took turns deciding which direction to turn and so on. We got on the tram and looked at each other, raising our eyebrows at each stop to ask whether the other person thought we should get off . . . still we weren't feeling very guided, so we got off at a stop and started walking in a direction.

We came to an intersection and somehow decided to go straight across. As we walked down the street, we realized there was no one on the street, so we should start knocking doors. We were next to the third door on the street, and right before knocking, we decided to return to the first door and start there, just to make sure we didn't miss anyone. No one answered at the first two doors, so we were quickly back to the third door, where we had originally decided to start knocking.

An elderly woman answered the door, and as we began to introduce ourselves she began to shut the door. I was struck by how kind she was trying to be. She hadn't slammed the door in our faces! Thankfully her daughter poked her head around the door to see who her mother was talking to before the door shut, and the daughter said, "These are people from the church that does family history." My companion and I looked at each other and quickly began to agree with the daughter, knowing full well that neither of us knew the first thing about doing family history in France or in general, but we sure wanted to keep that door open! The mother ended up opening the door to us, and we had a great lesson with an elderly couple and their grown daughter about many different aspects of our religion as well as their current religion.

By the time we had to leave they were asking when we would come back next—we were thrilled, to say the least, because it had turned into such a positive experience. That night my companion and I marveled at the tender mercies that led us to their door that day: our original plans and backup plans fell through; we weren't sure we were being led by the Spirit, but we were willing to move; we decided to knock doors when we got to their door; we didn't know anything about family history work, but we knew they knew our church. We later learned that they had seen elders help someone carry their groceries at least once, so we had multiple ways in their door, although we didn't know that at first.

We grew very close to that family, and the mother eventually became a member of the Church. Throughout the rest of my mission I stayed in contact with them. I love them as if I just left yesterday. . . . I was able to travel back to this area a couple of years after we met and it still felt as if we were dear friends as we relived many happy memories together.

Chapter 30

DON'T BE AFRAID

From the minute you enter the Missionary Training Center, you will practically never be alone for the next two years. There will always be someone there to support and guide you. Thousands upon thousands of full-time missionaries have served before you, and many thousands are now serving. Most of them entered their missionary service with the same concerns you may have. Of course, this is the first time you have served as a full-time missionary, but it is highly unlikely that your experience will be substantially different from that of those who have gone before. Your mission president and his wife will see that your needs are met. They will love you even before they meet you. You can rest assured of that.

If you are learning a new language, you can take great comfort in the fact that you were assigned and called by prophets of God to take on this challenge. It may seem impossible at first, but the language will come. As you are prayerful and diligent, you will be blessed with the gift of tongues. One of our missionaries was raised speaking Italian, then assigned to labor in France. He was taught French by English-speaking instructors and ended up learning both languages fluently. All of our Mandarin-speaking elders in France learned both Chinese and French, even when they had no knowledge of either language before their mission. Your language learning, like theirs, will be miraculous!

When I was anticipating my call to serve as a young man, the only hope I had was that I wouldn't be called to a French-speaking mission. I had taken French in school and had no further interest. When the call came and announced that I would be learning French, it came as a bit of a shock. Upon beginning my study at the Provo MTC, I quickly felt comfortable with the learning process and fell in love with the language. Ever since, I can sincerely say, "I love French!" What a surprise that would be for my junior high teacher!

Perhaps the most comforting fact of all is that the Lord will watch over you and protect you from day one. Your family and perhaps millions of others will be praying for you constantly. The Lord will hear those prayers and send blessings to you in ways you can't imagine. Occasionally, the will of the Lord for a particular missionary may be manifest in an early release from his mortal mission by accident or illness, to be continued on the other side of the veil.[1] This is extremely rare. You are much safer on a mission than you would be at home.

The Lord spoke to Joseph Smith and Oliver Cowdery in the earliest days of the Restoration, even before the Church was organized. He said, "*Fear not* to do good, my sons [and daughters], for whatsoever ye sow, that shall ye also reap; therefore, if ye sow good ye shall also reap good for your reward. Therefore, *fear not,* little flock; do good; let earth and hell combine against

1. Doctrine and Covenants 138:57.

you, for if ye are built upon my rock, they cannot prevail. Behold, I do not condemn you; go your ways and sin no more; perform with soberness the work which I have commanded you. Look unto me in every thought; doubt not, *fear not.*"[2]

The missionary force is no longer a "little flock." You will be part of a great army of the Lord, taking the gospel to every nation, tongue, and people. Look to the Lord, trust in Him with all your heart, and He will direct your way.[3] With a command and a promise, the Lord said, "Go amongst thy brethren, . . . and I will give unto you success."[4] "Go ye therefore, and teach all nations, baptizing them in the name of the Father, and of the Son, and of the Holy Ghost: Teaching them to observe all things whatsoever I have commanded you: and, lo, I am with you alway, even unto the end of the world. Amen."[5]

In Their Own Words

My companion and I were setting goals in my last transfer. I knew that I didn't have enough time to find, teach, and baptize someone before I went home, so I told my companion that my goal was to be a part of someone's conversion story. I wanted to work so hard and share my testimony of the gospel of Jesus Christ with as many people as I possibly could in my last few weeks as a full-time missionary. I did this, having faith that someone would come a little closer to Christ. It wasn't until two and a half years later that I received the following email: "Bonjour! I know you don't know

---

2. Doctrine and Covenants 6:33–36; emphasis added.
3. See Proverbs 3:5–6.
4. Alma 26:27.
5. Matthew 28:19–20.

me, but I just returned a few weeks ago from the Paris France mission where I served in Luxembourg for two transfers. I know your name because one of my favorite members there, a recent convert, mentioned you to me several times during my time there. She said that she was taught by lots of missionaries but never really "got it," if that makes sense, until you came to Luxembourg. She said there was just something different about you and she knew that it was something that she wanted. She said that it was you who really made her understand the importance of our message and that it would change her life for the better. I wanted to make sure you knew the influence you had on at least one person (and I'm sure plenty more). You are one of my mini-heroes I guess you could say. I hope you have a great day." I know that Heavenly Father is aware of our goals and always blesses us for our righteous desires.

EPILOGUE

Even now, several years after our release, I can see in my mind's eye the large display on the wall of the mission president's office in Le Vésinet, France. We called it the transfer board. It contained the picture of each missionary currently serving in the mission and those whom we anticipated coming in the near future. Oh, how we learned to love each of these young men and women and the senior missionaries who served with them. We still pray for them daily.

In the pictures taken for their mission applications, some of the missionaries look excited and confident. Some look a little frightened and unsure of themselves. Regardless of how they felt when that picture was taken, each one (and I mean *all* of them!) grew emotionally and spiritually in their selfless missionary service. Each one went home a better man or woman, a more devoted disciple of Jesus Christ, and far better prepared for the next phase of life.

You too will probably have some feelings of fear and inadequacy as you consider going on a mission. Set those feelings aside and go for it. You'll be just fine.

EPILOGUE

We often hear people speak of their service as "my mission." "When I was on my mission . . ." The truth is, it is not your mission. You are on the Lord's errand. It is His mission. The surgery doesn't belong to the scalpel. It's the surgeon's! The music doesn't belong to the piano. The instrument is just the servant of the musician. As a missionary, you will be the servant of the Master. If you let Him, He will make of you all you need to be. It is His work. He never fails. Neither will you, as you do it His way.

Follow the counsel of your mission president. Be faithful, obedient, and diligent. Listen to and follow the whisperings of the Spirit. Care for yourself and your companions. Love your investigators and all the people you meet. Your service as a full-time missionary will pass quickly, but it will be forever meaningful to you and those you serve.

May the blessings of the Lord attend you in your preparation, in your full-time service, and in all you do after returning home. Thank you for your willingness to serve!

"Therefore, if ye have desires to serve God ye are called to the work."[1]

---

1. Doctrine and Covenants 4:3.

A MISSIONARY'S PRAYER

Give me a mountain to climb, and give me a river to cross.
Grant me the fire to refine all the impure and the dross.

Give me some ground I can till, and give me the seed and the rain.
I'll plant by the light of Thy will, and consecrate all of the gain.

Fruit of my labors I yield to the God of the harvest, so kind.
Faith through my work is revealed with
all of my heart and my mind.

Father in Heaven, make of me all that Thy will can allow.
Then for all eternity, at Thy holy throne I will bow.

INDEX

INDEX

INDEX

Guidance, 67–71. *See also* Holy Ghost

Happiness, 125–27, 144

Heart: of missionary, 3; hardened, 48–50; teaching from, 97–98

Heroes, 63–65

Himni, 17

Hinckley, Gordon B.: on missionaries as Lord's tools, 101; on adulation, 134; companion of, 139

Holy Ghost: voice of, 9–13, 15–16; justification and companionship of, 24–25; and Foreign Object Debris, 43; language of, 72; and building testimony, 84; being led by, 87–88, 137–38, 144–46, 152–54; teaching with, 98, 99; speaking with help of, 127–29; gift of, as tenet of gospel, 150

Hope: in Jesus Christ, 50–51; defined, 54

Hugo, Victor, 5

Humility, 101, 130–31. *See also* Meekness

Immaturity, as obstacle to charity, 52–53

Inadequacy, feelings of, 101, 159

Individuality, 113

Investigators: understanding, when teaching, 37–41; helping, receive testimony, 84–87; searching for, 99, 109–10, 137–38, 144–46, 153–55; faith in finding, 131–32

Israelites, and brass serpent, 49–50

Jesus Christ: keeps promises, 19–21; faith in, 47–50; hope in, 50–51; becoming servant of, 52–53; calms storm, 79–82; calling upon, 82; teaching in name of, 98; power and authority of, 101. *See also* Atonement

Jet engines, 42–43

Joy, in work, 143–44

Justification, 22–26

Kirtland Temple, dedicatory prayer for, 100

Knocking, 67–71, 86

Lamoni, King, 9

Language: missionaries face discouragement due to, 19–21; and speaking with Holy Ghost, 127–29; and gift of tongues, 156–57

Learning, in wilderness, 121–23

Lee, Harold B., 85–86

Leslie (security guard), 32–35

Liahona, 44–45

Limits, self-imposed, 113–15

Love: for ourselves, 7–8, 16; for people you serve, 53; for companion, 73–76

McDonald, James, 57–58

McDonald, Sarah Ferguson, 57–58

McKay, David O., 15

Meditation, 14–15

Meekness, 98–99. *See also* Humility

Member missionary work, 109–10, 116

Military target practice, 106–9

165

INDEX

INDEX

ABOUT THE AUTHOR

Don H. Staheli serves as the secretary to the Quorum of the Twelve Apostles of The Church of Jesus Christ of Latter-day Saints. He previously served as the personal secretary to President Gordon B. Hinckley, as assistant secretary to the First Presidency, and as a Licensed Clinical Social Worker with LDS Family Services. He has fulfilled callings as president of the France Paris Mission, Regional Representative of the Twelve, stake president, bishop, and temple sealer, and he currently serves as a stake patriarch. He received a bachelor's degree in history and master's degrees in social work and international management. He is happily married to Cynthia Bodine Staheli. They have five children and twenty-one grandchildren.